WHERE SPEED IS KING

Also by Margaret O. Hyde

FLIGHT TODAY AND TOMORROW
DRIVING TODAY AND TOMORROW
ATOMS TODAY AND TOMORROW, New Rev. Ed.
EXPLORING EARTH AND SPACE, New Rev. Ed.
FROM SUBMARINES TO SATELLITES
MEDICINE IN ACTION
OFF INTO SPACE
PLANTS TODAY AND TOMORROW
ANIMAL CLOCKS AND COMPASSES

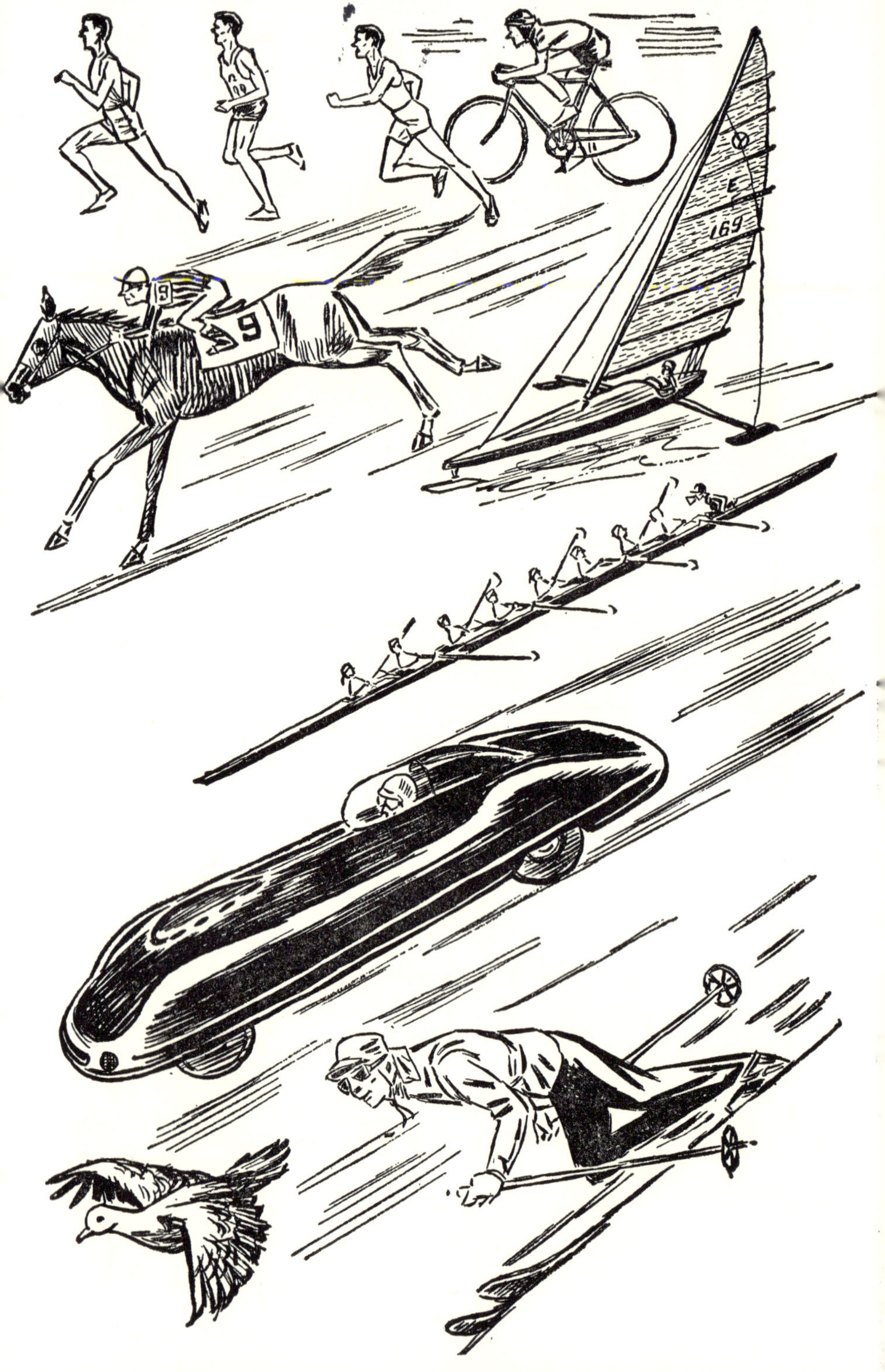
9
E
169

WHERE SPEED IS KING

Revised Edition

by MARGARET & EDWIN HYDE

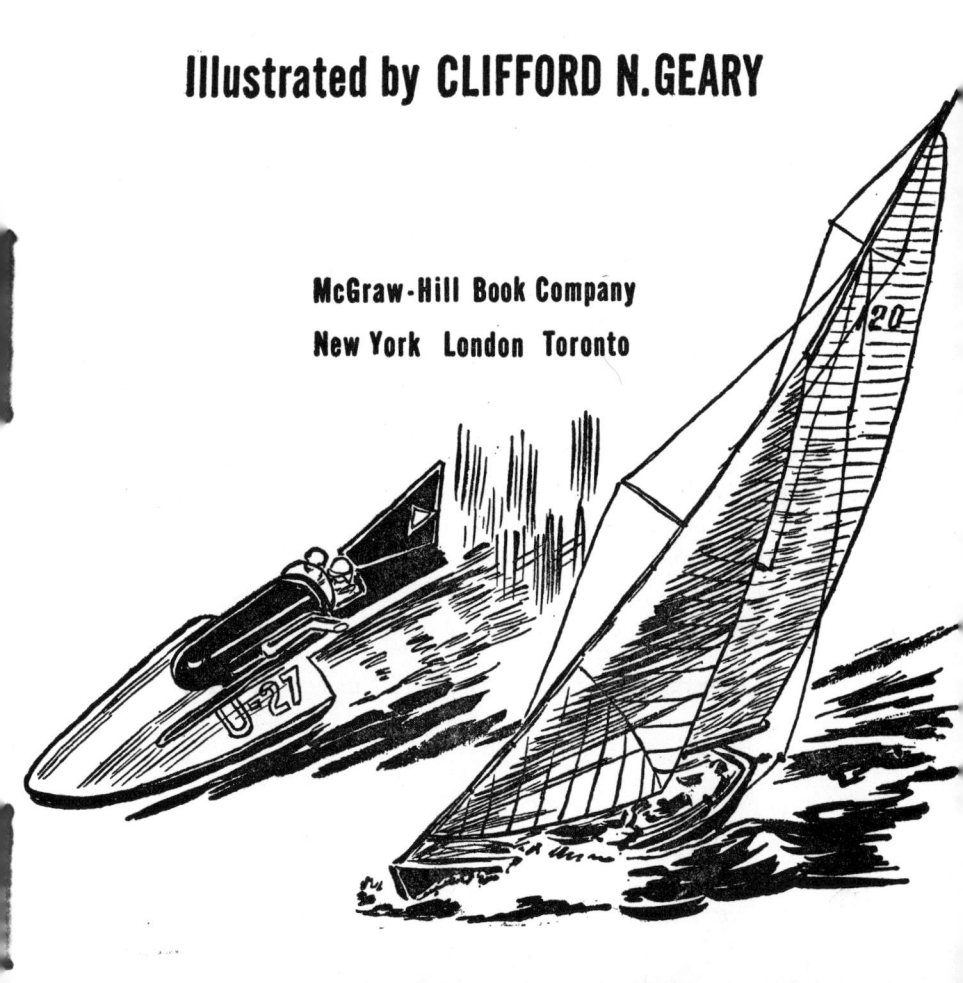

Illustrated by CLIFFORD N. GEARY

McGraw-Hill Book Company
New York London Toronto

ACKNOWLEDGMENTS

The authors wish to thank the many people who contributed information and suggestions for this book. The following were especially helpful: Hugo Biersach, American Water Ski Association; W. Van B. Claussen, Skate-Sailing Association; Dr. Thomas K. Cureton, Physical Fitness Laboratory, University of Illinois; C. O. Davis, Model Yacht Racing Association of America; Carroll F. Dorrell, Contest Board, American Automobile Association; Ethel M. Dassow, *The Alaska Sportsman;* Daniel J. Ferris, Amateur Athletic Union of the United States; C. Carroll High, Jr., Wright Air Development Center; Donald Horter, Island Heights Yacht Club; Carl Johnson, American Power Boat Association; Roger Langley, National Ski Association; C. S. Logsdon, National Aeronautic Association; Francis Ludwig, National Association of Amateur Oarsmen; Cora Lee Millenbach, International Renegade Ice Yacht Association; Carl R. Wheeley, Academy of Model Aeronautics; and personnel of the Medical Acceleration Laboratory, U.S. Naval Air Development Center, Johnsville, Pennsylvania.

The authors also wish to thank Robert J. Antonacci (Supervisor of Health, Physical Education, and Safety for the Gary, Indiana public schools; and co-author of *Sports Officiating,* and the *Young Champion* series of books) for his contribution to this revised edition of *Where Speed Is King.*

WHERE SPEED IS KING, Revised Edition

Copyright © 1961, 1955 by Margaret and Edwin Hyde. All Rights Reserved. Printed in the United States of America. This book or parts thereof may not be reproduced in any form without written permission of the publishers.

Eighth Printing

Library of Congress Catalog Card Number: 61-10134

07-031620-1

CONTENTS

Fastest Men in the World	7
Winter Carnival	17
Horses, Beautiful and Swift	44
Soap Boxes, Hot Rods, and Racing Cars	54
Boats in the Park	71
Sails at Full Speed	81
Fastest Boats Afloat	89
Pigeons That Race Home	101
Fun on Two Wheels	108
Fast Wings	122
Speeding Into Space	135
Official Sports Organizations	141
Index	143

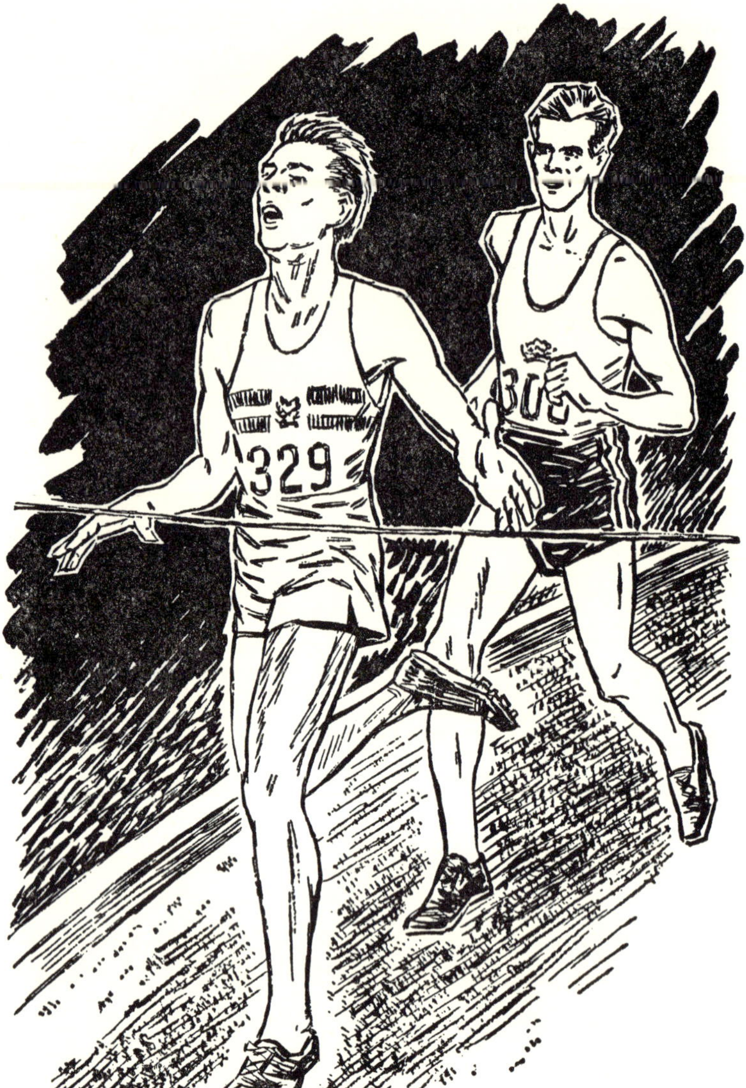
329

FASTEST MEN IN THE WORLD

THE TWO FASTEST men in the world ran into the last quarter of the greatest mile race in history amid a tremendous uproar of applause. The 32,000 spectators at the race were joined by millions who watched the spectacle on television. At this moment they were watching the greatest race of the twentieth century.

John Landy, Australia's world-record holder, was in the lead, setting a terrific pace which he hoped would be too fast for Roger Bannister's final burst of speed. But 90 yards from the tape, Bannister lengthened his stride and pulled himself up to Landy's heels. The crowd was almost hysterical as Landy looked over his left shoulder to see Bannister's position. Bannister was not there; he had come up to Landy. He pulled in front of him for a 4-yard lead and broke the tape to win the most exciting race in the history of track.

Never before had two men run the mile in less than four minutes in the same race. This happened on August 7, 1954, at the British Empire Games in Vancouver, Canada. Just three months before, Bannister had electrified the world by breaking the four-minute-mile barrier for the first time. On June 21, 1954, John Landy clipped 1.4 seconds from Bannister's world record in the cool twilight of Turku, Finland, running in the amazing time of 3 minutes and 58 seconds.

Since that time, many men have run the mile in less than 4 minutes. In March, 1959, Herb Elliott apologized for a time of 3 minutes, 58.9 seconds when he ran the mile in under 4 minutes for the eleventh time in less than a year. With today's faster tracks, better diets and training new records continue to be broken.

At one time, there were experts who believed man could not break the four-minute-mile barrier. Such speed is not just luck. For seven years, Roger Bannister drove himself toward the goal. For five years, Landy did the same. Both men disciplined their bodies to endure the punishment which comes with such racing. They learned how to draw every available bit of muscular power and nervous energy from their bodies, driving themselves on in spite of burning lungs and aching muscles which cried out from exhaustion.

Roger Bannister, as a medical student, had an opportunity to study the way his body reacted against strain. He experimented and studied ways of increasing the supply of oxygen to his body. He trained to make his heart better able to pump oxygen to his tissues. He learned to budget his energy so exactly that he is famous for his collapses which take place just after he hits the tape.

In the cases of both Landy and Bannister, bodies were trained to a peak. Both men keep themselves in excellent physical condition. Long periods of training and almost perfect conditions of track and weather enabled the men who followed them to break the four-minute-mile barrier. Herb Elliott's gruelling training enabled this Australian to set a new world record of 3:54.5 in Dublin in August of 1958. No one knows how fast men will run in the future, but it is certain that four-minute milers must be in top physical condition to meet such a fierce test of body and spirit.

Not long ago, many people believed that running was a dangerous sport and that many champions developed "athlete's heart" and died young. Some still hold to this idea, but a number of scientists have done experiments which seem to indicate that the opposite is true. Those who exercise wisely live as long as, if not longer than, the average person, and enjoy better health.

The term "athlete's heart" should be dropped from medical writing because, according to the *Journal of the American Medical Association*, it is used to describe a condition which probably does not exist. There is no doubt that hard running may injure hearts already weakened, but close examination of young athletes can identify those who should not participate.

Today many doctors believe that exercise, even when

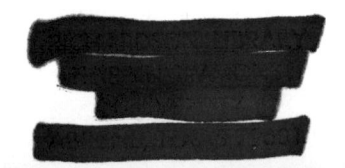

strenuous, will not damage a normal heart. Dr. Thomas K. Cureton, an expert in physical fitness, is among them. In his laboratory at the University of Illinois you might see famous athletes being tested in strange ways. One might be running on a treadmill with an oxygen mask clamped to his nose. Scientists are measuring the rate at which he is using oxygen and will make various tests on his circulation. Another man is diving down until he is under 7 feet of water. Scientists are waiting to measure the time which it takes for him to float to the surface so that they can tell what proportion of his weight is surplus fat.

You might see any of more than a hundred different tests being made on circulation, breathing, and fitness in this strange laboratory where physical fitness is being measured and evaluated. From the results of his tests, Dr. Cureton has made some interesting conclusions which may help you to enjoy better health for a longer time.

Studies show that normal boys and girls can improve

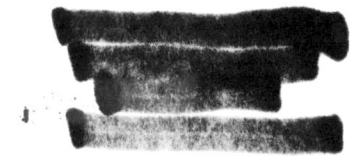

their health by running. Continuation of mild exercise for the years to come may lengthen life and cut down the chance of death from heart disease. Dr. Cureton believes that athletes keep their blood vessels constantly active and thus prevent them from thickening. The slow change which takes place in all human blood vessels is known as arteriosclerosis, or hardening of the arteries. Records show that athletes who remain active suffer from this change more slowly than those who practice a sedentary way of life. Actually, little is known about hardening of the arteries, and research shows that many factors contribute to the disease, but the time of onset might be later if a physical-fitness program is followed.

Dr. Cureton has traveled far and wide testing athletes. When he was in England in 1952, he tested Roger Bannister and recommended exercises to extend the efficiency of his body. Some believe that these gave Bannister the added stamina which enabled him to make the finishing spurt to victory in the Mile of the Century.

Perhaps you have hopes of becoming one of the fastest men in the world where records are tumbling year after year. If you have heard the roar of a crowd cheering you on to a faster pace as you run toward the tape at the finish line of a sprint or middle-distance race, you know something of the thrill of fast running. With better knowledge about pace, better coaching, improved running surfaces, and better running shoes, you may make better speeds. All of these, plus better diets, have enabled men to bring records lower and lower over a period of years. No one knows if the limit has been reached or will know when it is reached, because man will continue to strive for better speed.

If you think you have little chance of becoming a fast runner, you may be wrong. Few people use more than 25 per cent of their physical potential. If your doctor finds that your heart is normal and that you are in good physical condition, you can begin to strive for better speed today. If you have the urge to win and the determination to reach your goal, you may, after some serious training, surpass your highest hopes. You can begin by running, and running some more.

Natural ability helps a great deal, but good track men are the product of natural ability plus courage and training. Some of the champions have overcome tremendous physical handicaps. Cunningham, Bonthron, and San Romani were great runners who broke records in spite of leg handicaps. Recently, another runner became a champion in spite of a setback. Murray Halberg, a New Zealander, was injured in a game of Rugby football at the age of seventeen. His left side was paralyzed and his arm useless. At the age of twenty he broke the New Zealand record for the mile, with a time of 4 minutes 4.4 seconds. When the Mile of the Century was run, Halberg was one of the contestants, and only the best in the British Empire qualified for this race.

If you are under sixteen, you are probably not ready for long-distance running, but you may have qualifications which will enable you to join the sprinters. To do so, you need leg speed and fast reaction time. If you cannot manage a good starting technique, this is not the kind of racing for you.

If you can sustain sprinting speed over a long distance, you might excel in the quarter-mile races. Leg strength and endurance begin to count in such races, but speed is still the major requirement.

Middle-distance running, that is, all races over 440 yards and up to and including a mile, requires ability to judge pace as well as the possession of leg strength and speed. Some successful half-milers have had great strength and little speed, while others have had great speed and little strength. But all who excel in races longer than sprints have bodies which make efficient use of oxygen. Body builds vary, and so does running form, but there must be a mechanism which supplies enough oxygen to produce the energy needed for such running.

There have been so many spectacular mile races in recent times that a mile event has become the feature of many indoor and outdoor meets. Each runner plans his own strategy for a mile race, and those who compete in the outstanding events learn as much as possible about the type of race which their competitors usually run, so that they will know if they are running with fast pace setters or those who count on making fast sprints in the last lap. An inexperienced runner usually does best by setting a steady pace for himself and running each lap in the time he has set. Of course, it is very important to run "on the pole" (in the inside lane) so that you have less distance to cover. The man who stays in the second lane must run an additional 18 yards before completing the mile course. Before you can run a fast mile, you will need hard training and good coaching.

Relays are run at many different distances and have become so popular that they are sometimes the feature events of a track meet. Watching four good teams of men pass their batons, with some men picking up a few yards at the exchange because of their exact timing, is a thrilling experience. The race may be so close that positions change frequently, and excitement is high.

Relay runners may be specialists in their own fields. Some may be sprinters, others middle-distance or long-distance men. The latter are men who excel in competitions of two miles or more.

The long-distance runner must have a strong will and

the ability to drive himself after he reaches the tired feeling which precedes actual physical fatigue. Many experts believe that the endurance required for races of two miles and longer is too great for young runners.

In Europe, where a larger number of men continue running as they grow past college age, there are more outstanding long-distance runners, but the sport is increasing in popularity in the United States. Long-distance runners don't reach their peak until they are about twenty-five years old, so it is not surprising to find an older group of men running in the famous Boston Marathon. Although this 26-mile, 385-yard race from Hopkinton to Boston is usually won by mature runners, in 1951 a nineteen-year-old Japanese boy, Shigeki Tanaka, won the event with a time of 2 hours 27 minutes and 45 seconds.

Runners of all distances and ages can be seen each fall in the woods and open country. Cross-country running leads to better performance on the track and develops strength, which benefits all athletes.

Steeplechasing is a form of running which is especially valuable for hurdlers. This differs from cross-country running in the addition of obstacles such as hurdles and water jumps. You do not need a special track on which to practice. Babe Didrikson Zaharias, who practiced for the 80-meter hurdles by jumping over neighbors' hedges, won the event in the 1932 Olympics. Hurdlers must possess the speed of a sprinter, the endurance of a middle-distance runner, the spring of a jumper, and exactness of rhythm and timing. Whether the race is with low or high hurdles, the ease with which the runners jump over them is a pleasure to watch.

Another sport in which speed is king is swimming. This outstandingly healthful sport is a popular and important part of many school and club programs. There are many ways to have fun with speed in the water. Competitive races vary in distance from 40 yards to one mile, with younger, less experienced swimmers concentrating on the shorter distances. One specified stroke must be used in the races unless it is a medley race, which requires competitors to use three or four different strokes for certain distances. Relay races, retrieving races in which an object must be picked up and returned to the starting point, towing races, handicap races, and underwater races are just a few of the competitive events which swimmers enjoy.

As you train for better speed, try to improve your form and bring your body to top condition. Remember that you cannot become a champion in a few months or even a year. A good coach may need years to make you a champion, but great swimmers know that the reward is worth the effort. Consider yourself fortunate if you have the chance to have fun with speed in the water.

WINTER CARNIVAL

THE EXCITEMENT of winter-carnival weekend has spread through the whole community. Snow-sculptured statues stand majestically in front of the school. Visiting judges and teams fill the inn as fresh snowflakes add their beauty to the celebration.

After many weeks of careful preparation, everyone is eager for the program to begin. As soon as the snow is swept from the ice on the lake, speed will reign as king for the weekend.

Schedule of Events

Friday afternoon:

3 P.M.	Speed Skating
4 P.M.	Skate-sailing
7:30 P.M.	Winter Sports—TV Program
	Tobogganing
	Bobsledding
	Dog-sled Races

Saturday:

9 A.M.	Downhill Ski Races
10:30 A.M.	Cross-country Ski Meet
2 P.M.	*Slalom*
3 P.M.	Ice Yachting
9 P.M.	Carnival Ball

3 P.M. *Speed Skating*

The bright February sun casts soft, violet shadows on the white snow that covers the hills around the lake. A sharp wind whips across the ice, but crowds have gathered along the rope to watch the power and grace of the speed skaters who are listening for the starting gun. They are tense as they wait to rush forward at the exact moment the gun is fired. In this sprint race, as in all short ones, the start is important, for it is hard to pass the others once the action has begun.

At the crack of the gun, they lunge forward, and skate blades flash as the racers gain momentum with short jab strokes. Then with strokes that grow gradually longer and more graceful, they speed over the gleaming ice. Bodies are low, and arms are held across the slightly arched backs. There is barely a whisper as they glide down the straightaway.

The eyes of the spectators are turned toward number 9, who is in the lead. He sprints a corner, running the blades of his skates almost at right angles to the edge of the track. He is really skating sideways. You can hear the crunch which his blades make as they bite into the ice. Around he goes, forging ahead of the others, until he reaches the finish line first, covering the 220 yards in 20 seconds.

Number 9 is an expert at sprint racing. This top-notch speed skater might finish last in a 5-mile race, for each skater has his own speciality. Those training for short races emphasize starts and corners, while those who train for distance concentrate on endurance. But to skate with expert speed at any distance, you must train.

In addition to following the general training rules which are helpful to all sportsmen, these speed skaters begin special training in the fall to develop the muscle power of their legs by long walks and slow, easy runs. Many joined the school bicycle club, since bicycling uses many of the same muscles as speed skating.

When winter comes, the speed skaters are trim and ready for the biting wind and harsh demands that such competitions make on their bodies.

Today they speed with grace over the blue-white ice at a rate that is one of the fastest which man can attain under his own power. Race after race, skaters and spectators enjoy the thrill of this wonderful sport.

4 P.M. *Skate-sailing*

The sailors are ready for the next event. Many of the spectators have never seen skate-sailing, which is not a common sport in the United States, but it is one which offers safe speeding in the sections where there are frozen rivers and lakes. It is a sport which takes far less energy than speed skating, and were it not for the stamina and training required, it might be called a lazy man's sport. In skate-sailing the wind does most of the work. By properly carrying a suitably designed sail on his shoulder, a skater may travel at high speed over a frozen surface with little effort. In Scandinavian countries skate-sailing is sometimes a means of travel as well as a sport.

In addition to national championship races, cruising,

Winter Carnival

handicap, and novelty races are held under the sponsorship of the Skate-Sailing Association of America. Racing sails are limited in size to 1 square foot of area for every 2½ pounds of weight of person. If you weigh 150 pounds, your sail must not be larger than 60 square feet. Also, your blades must be no longer than 18 inches. Men and women compete on an equal basis, although occasionally there are special events for women.

Imagine yourself as one of the carnival team who prepare to race on this windy day. You have long racing skates on your feet and face the starting line holding overhead a kite-shaped sail which has been made of fine balloon silk stretched tightly on a cross frame of duraluminum spars. At the starting signal, you deftly snap the sail down so that the middle spar is resting on your windward shoulder. Now the wind strikes it at an angle, and off you go. You are leaning comfortably against the sail as you head for the first buoy at speed quickly approaching 50 miles per hour.

It is a full third of a mile to the first buoy of the triangular racing course. Zooming round the buoy at top speed, each racer settles down to speeding over the windward leg of the course according to his own best judgment. It is usually on this leg that races are won or lost. Skillful tacking, good judgment, sharp skates, and a tightly fitting sail that is expertly handled all contribute to gaining a lead position. Rounding the second buoy you settle down for the broad reach on the final leg of the course. Heeling your sail sharply into the wind, a maneuver unique and only possible in skate-sailing, you literally "ride your sail," with your skates hitting only the high spots in the ice, as you zoom along at close to 60 miles per hour to the finish line.

By the end of the afternoon everyone is exhilarated and ready for a good dinner, after which many gather by the fireplace at the inn to view a special telecast on winter sports. The white beauty of the Swiss Alps slips by as a train carries you to a Swiss resort where a toboggan chute is a popular attraction. You relax in your chair as a commentator describes the sport of tobogganing.

Tobogganing

The very old sport of tobogganing declined in popularity after the 1932 Olympics, when the enthusiasm for

Winter Carnival

skiing became so widespread, but, to many, tobogganing is still king of winter sports.

Part of the thrill of skiing is one's closeness to the surface over which he is speeding. On a toboggan a person is even closer to the snow than he is on skis. A toboggan is a sled without runners, usually made of strips of ash, maple, or hickory, with the front ends curled up. The bottom of the toboggan is highly polished, and on special tracks or chutes great speeds can be attained.

Imagine streaking downhill with your face just a few inches above the ice at a rate of 70 miles per hour. Those who cross the finish line at such speeds are the experts who practice on carefully prepared ice runs, such as this famous Cresta Run in Switzerland. Here, on a three-quarter-mile hill, there is a drop of 514 feet. Curves, banks, and leaps add to the thrills of those who race down from the top to the bottom in about one minute.

There are three sections to the run, the lower one being opened the first part of the season, then the second when the weather conditions permit, and then the top. One of the two famous annual races begins from Junction, a distance of 956 yards from the bottom. The second important annual race takes place at the end of the season from the top.

Try a race down the bottom section of the run. First you must put on knee and arm pads and a felt-lined crash helmet to protect yourself in case of accident. You must also put on special boots with steel spikes that can be used for steering and braking, for a toboggan is not equipped with a steering arm or a brake. Now you are ready to go.

Starting 10 feet behind the tape which is stretched across the run, you are off to a running start as you throw yourself flat on your sled and break through the starting line. This stops the clock which records your starting time. Keeping a straight course, with your body straight on the toboggan, your elbows tucked in, and your feet held up so they don't touch the ice, you are off.

Your toboggan seems to want to turn when it is traveling as slowly as this, and you must turn your body enough to correct the turning of the sled. Now you are about to hit the side of the track, but your padded elbow helps to straighten your course.

Faster and faster you speed down the run. Since you are new at this sport, you trail your feet to prevent the toboggan from zooming ahead at such a speed that you may not be able to control your course.

Now you are coming to a right corner. You prepare for it early by running to the left side of the course before you come to it, and as you reach it, you push yourself back on your sled. Now with your left hand forward and right hand back under your weight, you push the nose of the toboggan down slightly. Around you go to the right. At once, you return your right hand to its usual position and head straight down the course.

Next you must round a corner to the left. Your feet are still trailing to slow your speed, your toboggan is on the right side of the run, and your left hand is back. Now

Winter Carnival

the nose goes down and you are around the curve which bears to the left.

You come to a bend to the right, then a steep drop. Here you ride forward and keep to the center of the course. You are reaching the bottom of Cresta, you break the tape, and your time is recorded, but you are still speeding along. At the finish you go up the hill and turn to the left before you stop. Such a ride over the bottom section of Cresta would take less time than it does to read about it. Beginners often cover this distance in 40 seconds, and experts in as little as 30 seconds. But no matter what your time, or where your run, tobogganing is fun. Almost everyone knows that it is not necessary to have a run such as Cresta to have fun coasting. Wherever there is snow on a hill and a sled, there can be the thrill of sliding fast over the snow. Mile-long paths have been enjoyed by many who have discovered how to speed on a sled from one hill to the next, gaining speed as they go. Here, of course, the greatest danger is not from speed, but from crossing roads where automobile drivers may not see the sled coming or the sled riders not see the automobile, so it is wise to plan a course which avoids road crossing.

One modern way of enjoying a toboggan slide is to substitute a canoe for a sled. You can imagine the excitement of such a ride.

Bobsledding

From the toboggan run in Switzerland, the telecast takes you to Lake Placid, New York, and to the nearby Mount Van Hoevenberg bob run where thousands of passengers are thrilled each season by rides at speeds that seem as fast as lightning.

Bobsledding is America's only contribution to winter sports. It was introduced to Europe by an American in 1890 when he took a sled to Switzerland. The first run was built at Saint-Moritz, and many others followed.

The bobsled was developed by attaching runners to toboggans, thus giving them faster speed down hills of ice and snow. Steering and braking mechanisms provided better control.

Modern bobsleds can carry their crews close to 90 miles per hour at a height of 10 inches from the surface of the ice. Some of the sleds are steered by wheels, others by ropes. Some are made of wood, others are made of metal. Even the razor-sharp sled runners vary in length.

You will probably never buy a bobsled, but if you visit

Winter Carnival

the Mount Van Hoevenberg bob run, you might experience a thrilling ride on a sled maintained by the Conservation Department of the State of New York. These sleds are not as fast as the racing sleds used by experienced bobbers, but they are safer. Experienced drivers and brakemen take visitors down the run on a ride which many consider the most exciting of their lives.

As you watch sleds roar down the long run, gaining speed and zooming up the side of the wall on the curves, the announcer continues to supply information about the sport.

A fleet of forty sleds is ready for action when weather permits. Although the ride may seem terrificly fast and dangerous to the inexperienced, the Conservation Department of the State of New York takes every precaution to avoid accidents. The run is patrolled at all times to make certain that it is in perfect condition. From seven telephone control stations, men observe every foot of the slide. Before a sled may start, each one must report "all clear" to the starter. Then the bob begins its mile-long journey in which it will roar over twenty-six banked curves at a speed carefully controlled by the steersman and brakeman who make use of the sled's powerful brakes.

The Mount Van Hoevenberg bobsled run is coated daily during the winter season by spraying about 20,000 gallons of water over it from the nearby mountain streams which fill the storage reservoir. This is done so that the sled runners may bite in and hold the course. The straightaways have dirt under the ice and snow covering, but the curves are built of stone. The original cost of the run, which was built in 1930 for the Winter Olympics of 1932, was more than two hundred thousand dollars. The original cost of a racing bobsled may be over a thousand dollars and the upkeep of run and sleds is expensive. Bobsledding is far removed from simple coasting down a local hill.

Before a race a driver may be seen polishing runners or weighing himself with his crew on the official scales. Between races, crews practice their "bobbing" technique. You might see a crew sitting on a sled or even on the floor of a room following the commands of the driver. "Right," he says, and everyone leans to the right as far as he can. "Back" brings them to the neutral position, where they are sitting straight on the sled. "Left" they go, then "back" in unison as the driver calls his orders. This seems very simple, but one wrong move has sent many a crew trumbling from a sled which was speeding over the ice at a terrific rate.

The brakeman, who sits on the back of the sled, directs practice of the "bob." Everyone is leaning back until they are almost lying flat when he orders, "Bob!" At once they bend forward to an upright position. When a bobsled is crackling down a long straightaway, such actions make the sled speed forward at such a rate that it almost jumps ahead.

Some of the racers prefer to make a smooth run, taking the corners wide, while others feel that they gain time by skidding corners and bumping the sides of the track.

To arrive safely at the bottom in near record time, a crew must be well trained, and the driver and brakeman must be well skilled in their arts.

Such a crew is about to race against time. The crowd is tense, for each run on a racing sled is dangerous and breath-taking. More than one sled has climbed too high on a curve, bringing one or more of the crew to tragedy, but racers continue to smash down the bob runs.

The sled is towed toward the starting line, and the four helmeted crewmen stand in their places next to it. They rock the sled back and forth in the tracks of previous sleds, then give one great push and the sled is in motion. They run along beside it, pushing as hard as they can for a flying start. The driver jumps in and the crew take places behind him, each one pushing until he climbs aboard. Faster and faster they zoom down the run, riding high on the almost perpendicular walls of curves. Everyone but the driver rides with his head down, eyes shut, hanging on tightly to the man ahead. Men in booths along the run keep the crowd posted by means of a public-address system. Soon after the sled flashes across the finish line, the time is computed and announced. The 5,013 feet of the run have been covered in 1 minute 15 seconds. This is excellent time, but there are three more heats to be run against the other teams, and no one knows what the final result will be. Sometimes a few hundredths of a second may mean the difference between winning and losing.

Those who race with the hope of establishing a new record, those who prefer a safer ride on slower sleds, and those who watch agree that bobsledding is an exciting sport.

Dog-sled Racing

The next telecast is a film about dog-sled racing.

Howling wind may roar over the snow and ice and temperature may be far below zero, but the whole town turns out for the thrill when mushers race their dogs. Through the long, bleak Alaskan winter, men and dogs train and race. At Sun Valley, Lake Tahoe, and in Quebec, at the New England Championship in New Hampshire, the American Dog Derby in Montana, the Alaska Championship in Anchorage, and many other places, dogs are the heroes of the race.

The most famous of all is the North American Dog

Racing Championship at Fairbanks, Alaska, which is held each year early in March. Almost every Alaskan village, large or small, has held races before the big event. Championship teams from Alaska and farther away gather for the wonderful spectacle. Many teams arrive by air, and the excitement mounts as arrangements are completed before the opening day of the three-day race.

There are harnesses and sleds of many varieties and dogs of a number of breeds, but every driver must enter a minimum of five dogs. He may include as many dogs as he wants, but all that start in any race must cross the finish line in front of or on the sled. Most drivers use at least nine dogs the first day and drop one or two from the team on successive days.

No matter what the number of dogs, dog-sled racing is one of the toughest competitions in sports. The physical demands on the driver are terrific, and the patience required to train a good lead dog is more than many can imagine. But a good leader and his driver are close friends, and no matter how many dogs are replaced on a team, the lead dog never changes. He must be the toughest and the fastest runner of them all and one who is intelligent and obedient to the driver's commands. He need not pull, but he must break trails, make the turns, and buck the bitter wind.

After four of five months of intensive training, all the dogs and the driver have learned to work as a unit and are ready for the toughest race.

Before the big races begin, radio broadcast points are

set up along the course. Long before the starting signal sends the first team down the chute, huge crowds gather to watch the impatient, howling dogs. One by one the teams line up in starting positions according to numbers which the drivers drew before the opening day. Flash bulbs explode as photographers snap the favorites, and the tension increases.

But the drivers must appear calm so that the dogs do not sense their nervousness. Each dog on the team must be at his best. Each driver aims to break a record, to win for the thrill of winning and to capture the first prize, which may be well over two thousand dollars. This is the day for which a driver has trained his dogs. Keeping calm, or at least acting so that the dogs do not sense the tension, is not easy for a musher, especially in the midst of a noisy crowd after months of working alone.

Twenty-five teams will start at three-minute intervals. The driver hears his number and his team takes its place at the starting line. A microphone is put in front of him for a quick interview, while other men help him to hold the eager dogs. The seconds are counted and the starting gun flashes. The driver gives his command to his dogs. This may be "Mush," "Yake," "Hike," or just "All right." The dogs will obey any starting command used regularly by their driver. The exact word does not matter; it's the training and the teamwork that count.

Amidst the cheers, Driver Jeff and his team speed through the starting chute and lunge forward on the trail. The fourteen yelping Siberian Huskies stretch out

44 feet in front of the sled pulling strongly at a rapid pace. The only control is the commanding voice of the driver. No brake could stop them by its force, but the dogs would respond quickly to its grinding noise and a "Whoa" from Jeff.

"Haw" sends the team to the left, and "Gee" to the right, and "Haw come in" means to turn around. When the occasion arises, "Down" will bring the team to a sitting or lying position. No matter what the command, the dogs have been trained to obey.

Many mushers resort to various tricks in training their dogs for extra speed. Some dogs who have been trained to chase airplanes run as though they were trying to pull the plane from the sky. Jeff's team has been taught to give an extra burst of speed when it sights game, but it does not leave the trail. In perfect obedience, it rushes on without turning to complete the chase.

As the team runs along the course, Jeff cracks a whip and calls, "Pick it up." When they reach a sudden curve, Jeff steps off the sled runners and runs behind. On the downgrade, he slows the speed of the sled by dragging the soles of his shoes to prevent it from piling up on the dogs ahead.

The pace is steady and the speed is good, good enough to overtake the team ahead. Jeff signals to pass, and the first team must stop, according to the rules, and wait until Jeff's dogs and sled are in front of them. This rule does not hold when they are in sight of the finish line.

The 20 miles are covered in less than an hour and a half, and Jeff's tired team crosses the finish line. Two more days of racing will follow, with courses 25 and 30 miles in length. The winner will be the team that shows the best total time for all three days of racing.

The North American Championship Dog Derby is a race for the best mushers in the country. Less important races offer excitement for the amateurs. Women and girls race dogs, too, and young boys begin as early as six years of age to ride the sleds. The Alaskan Sled Dog and Racing Association sponsors a junior racing club in Anchorage.

Whether you are six or sixty, you can have fun as a dog musher *if* you have the dogs, snow, the endurance, and the patience.

The first day of winter carnival is over, and everyone is ready for a good night's sleep. Many who will participate in the ski races have gone to bed early after giving their skis a good coat of lacquer. Wax will not be applied until morning, for no one knows what snow the night will bring.

9 A.M. *Ski Races*

The second day of winter carnival dawns bright and

clear. All the racers are refreshed this morning after a long night's sleep and are ready for the vigorous fun ahead. They all know that physical and mental fitness play a big part in determining a winner.

The morning trace of mist hangs over the white valley while skiers check bindings, poles, and skis to make certain that they are in perfect order. By nine, you can feel the excitement of the race which is about to begin.

Each contestant has developed an eye for the country and cool, calculating judgment. He stands at the starting line and pictures in his mind the straightest safe course from top to bottom of the downhill run, for the straightest is the fastest. Some skiers will risk the hard places straight, while others will be more conservative and count on getting there more safely. They can take many curves in the time it takes a man to recover from a spill.

One by one, the racers are started at minute intervals, using standard racing crouch. Down they roar, with perfect control and grace, over the brilliant white snow.

The onlookers cheering at the finish line eagerly await the official results, for the first one may not be the winner, since total time from start to finish must be figured. A difference of seconds may determine the winner, but win or lose, the downhill race is a thrill to all who arrive safely at the bottom and all who watch the experts ski it.

Obstacles may be placed along the course of a downhill run. Artificial bumps, ruts, and steep drops may be added to make the downhill race the most dangerous and exciting of all kinds of ski racing.

It is 10:30 A.M. and time for the next event, the cross-country, or long-distance, ski race. This is a measure of endurance as well as of skill on skis, but no artificial obstacles may be included. About one-third of the course is downhill, one-third over level ground, and one-third uphill. Red flags and red rags tied around trees mark the course. Ski patrol, volunteers who have trained to help in emergencies, are posted at intervals along the trail which has been skillfully laid. Along with an interesting change of scene, the cross-country skier finds ample chance to demonstrate his ability on turns, on climbs both uphill and down over obstacles. Over open spaces and through the woods, with magnificent speed and grace, so that they seem barely to touch the snow, the skiers streak by, one after the other.

Some racers are reaching the end, but the first one at the finish line is not necessarily the winner. Starting time must be considered. Last-minute spurts are made by a few; others seem just able to drag to the end.

Two members of the ski patrol are bringing in the casualty, number 8, who straddled a tree near the finish line. The thousands of spectators who stand on both sides of the course groan as he is carried past them. But as soon as the bruises are healed and broken bones are mended, number 8 will be back in line giving others dramatic competition.

At two o'clock in the afternoon comes the *slalom*, a third type of ski race. The *slalom* is a race which tests the technical skill of a skier over a course which imitates some of the difficult situations encountered on wooded trails. Such a zigzag race downhill demands complete control of all turns and perfect coordination of body and skis.

Slalom courses are set in special ways; they are not just pairs of flagged poles set here and there. Setting a good *slalom* course is an art which is developed with lots of experience. A course which may be run in sixty seconds may be the product of many hours' work on the part of the course setter. And the skier may have practiced for many years to be able to judge the turns with split-second timing. One inch may mean a spill; one second may lose the race.

To begin his training, the *slalom* racer usually sets a few pairs of flags, called gates, on a slope and practices going through these until he can turn very close to the flag, an exercise which makes his path as nearly a straight line as possible.

As many as sixty pairs of poles, with red, yellow, and blue flags, are placed about 3 feet apart in different patterns. Circles of ink on the snow around each pole help to make the position of the flag a more permanent one even if it should be knocked down by a skier.

In giant *slaloms*, flags are placed farther apart, races are set over longer courses, and greater speed is attained.

No contestant may run through the gates before the race, but each one pictures his course in his mind as he climbs the hill. By memorizing the groupings, he maps his course, so that he knows at which speed and angle he can run each gate.

One by one, the racers push off at the starting gate. After a few short strokes with his poles, the skier uses them again only when he whizzes through the very narrow gates. Each contestant streaks down the hill with grace in spite of the twisting course. Here and there one is penalized for straddling a flag or for shooting right past a pair of gates instead of running through them.

Those who reach the finish tape in the shortest time may thank their luck, but their success is due largely to long hours of practice, to perfect technique, and to superior judgment. A winner must know just how to enter a gate so that when he leaves he will be in the best position for the following pair.

Many find *slalom* racing such fun that they buy specially made skis which are slightly narrower than those made for regular downhill racing. Even those who just watch see beauty in a well-set course, with its colorful flags waving high above the white snow, ready for action.

Slaloms are followed by skijoring, a variation of racing on skis for those who crave more speed. Skijoring is a race on ice- or snow-covered roads, in which skiers are pulled by horses. This is not a sport for beginners, for great skill is required to control both the horse and one's skis. This is especially true at corners.

With one hand, the skier grasps a bar which is connected to the horse's collar, and with the other hand he grasps the reins. Racers travel over a marked course at great speed. Here, as in the case of many kinds of racing, the skill at corners often determines the winner.

For those willing to risk greater danger, there is a variation of skijoring in which skiers are towed across a frozen lake by an airplane. Here the skier must not only be able to handle his skis expertly; he must know when to let go of the rope so that he does not rise with the plane.

3 P.M. *Ice Yachting*

Very few at the winter carnival want to risk the dangers of skijoring, but many iceboat enthusiasts spent last evening sharpening the runners of their boats for the dangerous sport of whipping across the frozen lake in their highly polished yachts. Competition will be keen and speeds several times faster than the wind after the starting gun opens the regatta.

While crowds gather at the edge of the lake, each skipper checks the rigging to make certain that he has adjusted it properly to make the most of the weather conditions and to assure his safety. Many of the skippers have made all necessary alterations themselves, not trusting anyone else with the responsibility. A mistake might mean a spill, and at high speed injury or even death might result.

Off they go. Blades gleam like silver in the sun as the boats leap ahead on the glasslike ice. An airplane flies above with a timing device to clock the boats as they travel over the diamond-shaped course. The wind is 25 miles an hour, and some of the yachts are reaching speeds nearly five times this great. Skippers strain every muscle to keep boats under control. They must rigidly obey the rules for right of way, since a wrong move at such speeds could spell disaster.

In spite of the hard work, the biting winds, and the danger, these speed kings of the ice enjoy their sport. Class after class, they skim along at breath-taking speeds. Most of the boats are E-class skeeters, but three A-class yachts are competing today. Each of the three costs between three and six thousand dollars and is between 50 and 70 feet in length. Most skippers are between the ages of twenty and fifty, but one event features a race for juniors, each in a specially designed boat costing about five hundred dollars. No matter what class boat a skipper owns, he is much too tired by the end of the competition to join those who put on ski boots and skis for an afternoon of skimming over the snowy slopes.

You need not be an expert to enjoy the fun of skiing. The hiss of your boards over the powdery snow, the glow on your face from the crisp fresh air, and the beauty of snow-decked trees and blue sky will give you a wonderful feeling, no matter how fast or how slowly you travel. You may never reach the skill of the racing kings, but in a short time you can speed downhill at a rate that is fun for you, and you will feel as though you are going just as fast as the best.

Millions of skiers swarm down snow-covered hills from Maine to Oregon each winter. They range in age from a few years to many, including older ones who are beginners. Some play on little hills, others take the ski lifts to mountaintops. Their speeds vary, but to each, his own speed is a thrill.

Here and there, throughout the country, competitions are held on the racing trails. Here the serious skiers attain magnificent speeds with scarcely any movement of their bodies. They travel the well-manicured trail with grace, so that many who watch cannot resist the desire to imitate them. But expert skiing takes much training and practice.

Many free ski schools turn out thousands of new skiers each year through mass instruction programs. Several small towns are training young skiers with such enthusiasm that they are producing some outstanding racers. For example, at Steamboat Springs, Colorado, skiing is part of the school curriculum on an elective basis. The program is arranged to provide fun and exercise, opportunities for good sportsmanship, and a good skiing background to all who wish to participate. Those students who show the qualifications necessary to become experts may become champions at an early age. Andy and Dave Lawrence are fine examples of this. These young people from Steamboat Springs rate with the best in the country.

Winter Carnival

The champions of the winter carnival will receive their prizes at the carnival ball. Winners, losers, and those who just watched have enjoyed a weekend of snow, ice, and speed.

HORSES, BEAUTIFUL AND SWIFT

OPEN GATES in the whitewashed fence welcome you to an immaculate horse farm. This spring the baby horses, or foals, have been born, and you can see them standing in the field close to their mothers. The one, Andy, is an especially beautiful chestnut thoroughbred who might become the miracle of speed, stamina, and courage which is typical of champions. No one knows what his future might be, but his owner has high hopes.

Now Andy spends most of his time resting and running around the paddock with his mother. You can see him nibbling grass, with his long legs spread far apart and his short neck reaching down next to his mother. He still depends largely on his mother's milk for food, but he is gradually developing an appetite for grain and grass.

Just after Andy was born, he stood up on his wobbly legs and took a few uncertain steps before he rested close to his mother. During his very first day, the trainer talked to him in a soft voice so that he would not fear people as he grew older. Day after day, he had fresh water and was rubbed, curried, and brushed. Day after day, he enjoyed romping and playing in the soft grass.

When Andy was about two weeks old, his trainer placed a little halter on him and taught him to walk beside his mother when she was taken out to pasture. This was just the beginning of his schooling, for a good race horse must learn manners.

At six months, Andy will be separated from his mother and put into a paddock with other colts and fillies. At this stage he will be called a weanling. He will soon learn to care for himself, but both his owner and trainer will continue to watch over him carefully through the months to come. Much thought and care were given to this horse even before he was born. His owner studied blood lines for many months before choosing the parents of this new horse which he hopes will be a winner when his turn comes. He is bred to be a champion. Breeding is only part of the story, but it is an important part.

All thoroughbreds are originally descended from one of three Arabian stallions which were brought to England early in the eighteenth century and mated with English mares. This was the beginning of the thoroughbred breed. Andy's parentage, name, and other information about him will be registered with the American Jockey

Club in New York City, where records are kept of every thoroughbred horse in the country. About six thousand horses are added to the books each year.

Every horse born during this year will become one year old next January, the universal horse birthday. Andy was born in March, but he will be considered one year old in January. Then he will be a yearling.

While Andy grows ready for the summer sale of yearlings, he will play and eat and sleep. He will continue his schooling, too, learning to be calm around people and to love those who work with him. He will learn to be mannerly when the blacksmith trims his feet each month. He will learn to walk quietly into a horse van so that when the time comes for transportation from stable to race track he will be willing to enter a van. His trainer will work slowly and patiently, for all young horses are timid. The trainer knows that it may take long hours to make the horse forget something which has frightened him. Andy will learn to walk near places where there are automobiles and crowds of people, so that he will become accustomed to them long before he meets them at a race track.

In the spring, information about Andy will be sent to a company which conducts sales of yearlings for listing in the catalogue. When sale time comes, he will be shipped to a paddock where many other horses gather for the same experience. Yearling sales are exciting times. No one knows the true value of the young horses, so there are bargains every year. On the other hand, some horses which sell for high prices because of their breeding make a poor record on the track. These horses become known as "lemons."

People from all walks of life will gather at the yearling sales and look at Andy when he is led into the ring under the spotlights at the time of his auction. The auctioneer will read a record of his breeding and of the races won by his parents.

Bids for the average horse run about $1,500. Andy is an especially fine horse, so he may bring far more for his owner. Some horses of famous background have sold for $50,000 and even more. Many earn far more than their purchase price while others do not. Because no one knows what will happen and because so much money is involved in buying and training horses, horse racing has become known as the "sport of kings."

Perhaps you are wondering why it is so difficult to select a winner when the breeding is so carefully recorded and presented. Nervous energy, courage, temperament are traits which are hard to recognize at this time and under sale conditions. Breeders do everything possible to encourage the yearlings to be mannerly at sales.

After the yearling sales, the owner will select a name and register it with the Jockey Club. Andy will be "broken" to the saddle by his new trainer. He may be led around the ring with just the weight of a trainer's hand on his back until he becomes accustomed to this. He may be blindfolded in his stall while a light boy climbs on his back, gently and carefully. His eyes are covered so that the sight of the action will not frighten him and his first saddle will not have stirrups to swing about and frighten him.

The breaking in of a horse like Andy is usually an easy process, far different from the wild excitement associated with wild West rodeos.

Quietly and gently Andy will be led out of the stable with a boy on his back and will walk round and round until he is accustomed to saddle, bridle, and the weight of the boy. The presence of other horses with riders usually helps to reassure the yearlings. The group will be led behind a boy on a pony which acts as a schoolmaster and will learn to answer the pressure on the reins. Then they will go into a ring or paddock and learn to walk, trot, and gallop slowly.

Yearlings have their school early in the morning. For many, the learning process takes only a few weeks before they are ready for the race track. After they have learned to gallop, they learn to gallop "on the rail," on the outside of several horses, and between two other horses. Together they enjoy the wonderful rhythm of running, the excitement of pounding down the stretch faster and faster, the glorious feeling which comes with the race. Here they learn to satisfy the craving for speed which has been bred into them.

As soon as Andy is fit, probably in his second spring, he will gallop a half mile, then try gradually longer distances. He will still be shy and nervous and may need a great deal more schooling before he is ready to race amidst all the noise and excitement that come with the crowds of people on race days. He will race many times in front of the professional horsemen who will clock him with their stop watches. He will learn to stand quietly by the rail while other horses thunder past him. His exercise boy will talk to him to steady and soothe him and to make him obedient. Andy will learn to understand the tones of his voice and to respond accordingly.

When Andy has learned to race straight and true and to respond to the commands of his exercise boy, he will be confronted with the problem of the starting gate. To a two-year-old horse, such a contraption probably looks like a monster, but he must learn to break from the starting gate before he can graduate from his early-morning school. At first, Andy will be walked around the gate and through it several times while his exercise boy talks to him to calm his nervousness. He is high-strung and bursting with energy. Sometimes he must be coaxed, sometimes gentled and then prodded. When he feels at home near the gate, he will be locked in one of the stalls for a few minutes before the doors are quietly opened again. This lesson will be repeated until he has no fear of his little prison. Next he will learn to leave the gate fast and straight as the gates open and the starter's bell clangs.

When Andy has graduated from the training school, he will be ready to begin his racing career, trying his speed and courage against other two-year-olds. He will probably sense the real race day, and the excitement

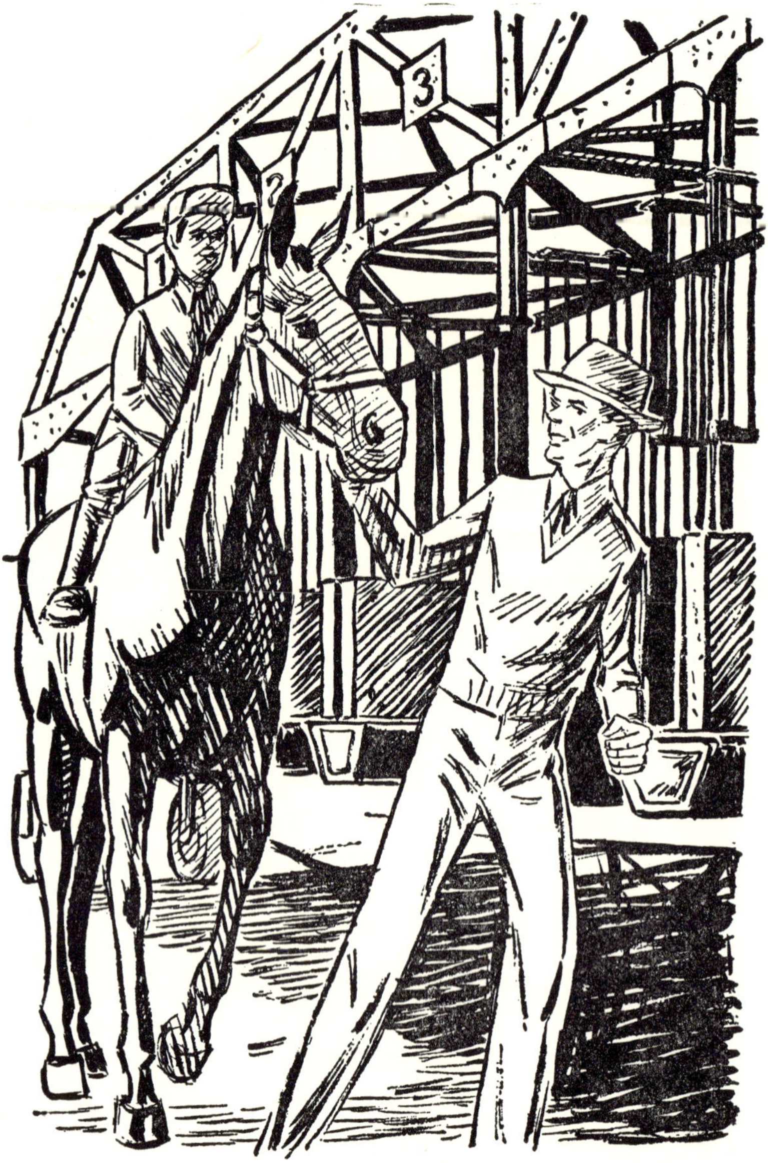
1
2
3

of his first post parade will make him more nervous than usual, but Andy is a horse full of fire and spirit for competition. He may be a champion on some of the finest tracks such as Belmont, Santa Anita, and Hialeah.

There are over a hundred thoroughbred race tracks in the United States, to which millions of people come each year. Some enjoy the beauty of the satin-coated thoroughbreds and the excitement of the races, while others are interested mainly in the betting, a phase of horse racing which has made it unpopular with many who are against all kinds of gambling. Although racing is dependent on the willingness of wealthy men to invest in the breeding and training of thoroughbred race horses, many kinds of people gather at the tracks to join in the suspense of race day. Many become so devoted to their favorite horses that for the short time of the race they feel like owners. Those who pick Andy will roar as his colors flash into sight and he thunders down the stretch and into the lead before plunging under the wire. They will cheer him as he walks to the judge's stand and into the winner's circle. Andy will be their horse when the horseshoe of roses is put around his neck. But Andy has a long way to go before he reaches his running prime at the age of three and four years.

If he runs well in the years which follow, he will retire in honor to the stud farm to reproduce his speed and courage. He may father thoroughbreds which will race as he did, and he may produce some who will have the characteristics which make them steeplechasers. Such horses are usually larger and rangier and have extremely powerful legs and shoulders. They must show outstanding jumping ability and stamina but need not be as fast as flat racers.

Steeplechasing is racing over a course on which there are obstacles such as hedges, fences, and water holes. Such jumping races are held at some of the major tracks, but in many cases they are events at the private hunt clubs where owners are the jockeys. Expert horsemanship is required in steeplechase racing, and the danger from spills is great. Sometimes both horse and jockey are hurt.

Andy will not produce any trotters or pacers. These horses, who run in a third type of racing known as harness racing, are a different breed, the standardbred.

These pictures will help you to see the difference between trotting and pacing. A trotter's diagonal feet, that is his right front and left rear, come down together. A pacer uses both legs on one side at the same time. The man or woman who rides in the small light carriage behind a trotter persuades his horse to trot or pace at full speed without breaking into a gallop. The little carriages are known as sulkies.

Harness racing has increased greatly in popularity within the past ten years. About a hundred new harness-racing tracks have been built in that time, with night races attracting crowds of people. Drivers of the sulkies range in age from twenty to eighty; many are farmers, and

Horses, Beautiful and Swift

a few of the favorites are women. Harness racing is an American sport. The most famous event in the world of harness racing is the Hambletonian, which is run each year at Du Quoin, Illinois.

No matter what the kind of racing, "They're off!" means excitement to the crowds who love fast horses.

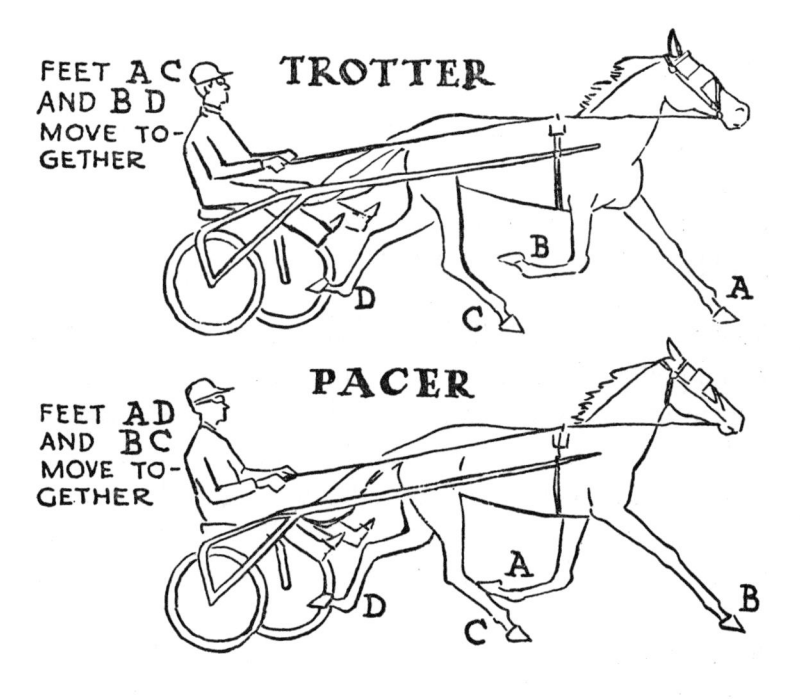

TROTTER
FEET A C AND B D MOVE TOGETHER

PACER
FEET A D AND B C MOVE TOGETHER

SOAP BOXES, HOT RODS, AND RACING CARS

THE NOSES of three little cars are pressed against the metal plates which prevent them from rushing down the course at Derby Downs. Ahead of them lies a downhill, concrete racing strip which is 975 feet long. It is coated with green paint to cut down the glare, and lined with silver to show the lanes. A yellow dotted line is painted down the center of each lane to guide the driver.

Three drivers sit proudly in the cars at the starting line. Their ages range between eleven and fifteen, for they are drivers of soap-box racers that have won local races. Each one has come from hundreds of miles away with his car to compete in the All-American Soap Box Derby in Akron, Ohio. This all-expense trip is one of their rewards for building superior cars and showing outstanding racing skill. Bigger prizes are ahead for today's winners, including scholarships ranging in value from a thousand dollars to five thousand dollars.

Race day dawned bright and hot, but the drivers barely notice the weather. The 60,000 people who fill the stands at the edge of the course are just a blur to them. Each helmeted driver is thinking only of the race ahead.

Tension mounts as the starting lever is released, the metal baffle plates drop even with the track, and the cars go speeding forward. They reach a speed of 26 miles per hour, getting to the finish line in less than half a minute. They whiz under the three-decker steel bridge where an electric eye and photo-finish camera equipment aid the judges overhead.

The first of the three boys qualifies for another heat, but two are ushered from the end of the runway to the losers' paddock where they can watch the rest of the race. For a few minutes, they are too disappointed to notice the three little cars which come speeding down the runway every sixty seconds. But before long, they can cheer the winners. They are local champions who are good sports, who ran a fair race and had a fine time at the "greatest amateur racing event in the world."

Three million people enjoy the sport of building or watching soap-box racers each year. If you want to join the boys who compete for places in the All-American Soap Box Derby, ask your local Chevrolet dealer for an official rule book.

All over the country boys work after school and on

Saturdays building cars within the ten-dollar cost limit. They study streamlining, draw plan after plan, and build fine cars using official soap-box wheels and axles. They make certain that steering wheels are firmly attached to steering shafts and that brakes meet with safety regulations.

Here are some tips which may help you win.

Keep the center of weight as low as possible without getting nearer than the 3 inches to the ground which clearance rules demand.

Over-all balance of the car is important in soap-box racers, just as it is in automobiles. Distribute the weight in your racer so that each wheel carries an equal amount when you are in the driver's seat. To check wheel balance, make a chalk mark on the outside of each wheel. Note where wheels stop in relation to the chalk mark. A well-balanced wheel will stop at a great variety of places, but one which is not properly balanced will stop with the heavy section down.

Actual downhill practice will help you to drive straighter. Measure and mark a straight line down a local hill and learn to follow it. Since a straight line is the shortest distance between the start and the finish, learning to drive straight is an important step in the training of a winner.

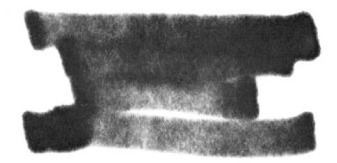

Keep wind resistance as low as possible by sloping the hood and cowl and by making the car's surface completely smooth. This means getting rid of any bumps from nailheads, screwheads, and the like. Paint and lacquer your racer and polish it until it shines like glass.

Win or lose, you'll be proud of your car and enjoy one of the best sports in which speed is king.

Next year some of the soap-box drivers will graduate to cars with motors. Many have been waiting impatiently for drivers' permits and have enrolled in the driving courses at their high schools. In addition to becoming expert drivers of the family car, some hope to participate in the races which are sponsored by local hot-rod clubs that are under the direction of civic and school administrators. Members of clubs which are affiliated with the National Hot Rod Organization agree to a strict membership code and try to live up to their motto, "Dedicated to Safety." Their drag meets are endorsed by some of the nation's foremost insurance companies, and their actions are quite different from those of the "shot rods" who are the cowboys of the highway.

Drag races are competitions in which two cars race against each other or in which one races against time. Classification of cars helps to make the races fair. For instance, stock cars run against stock cars, dragsters against dragsters. About twenty-six classes are recognized. Careful planning and checking help to make them safe. No sanctioned races are run on highways unless they have been roped off by police or abandoned. Unused airstrips and dry lakes are the scenes of many of the drag meets.

The major speed contests of the National Hot Rod Association are held for a week each summer the week before Labor Day on the Bonneville Salt Flats in Utah. Imagine a vast expanse of dry, hard-packed salt stretched out under a gleaming sun. This smooth surface of 150 square miles is an ideal place for fast, safe driving, and it is here that the fastest driving in the world has been done. When John Cobb sped 394.2 miles per hour at Bonneville in 1947, the speed record for the flying mile was multiplied by ten in comparison with the record of forty-nine years before.

On September 9, 1960, Mickey Thompson, an American, took his sleek blue streamliner, Challenger I, boosted it to 406 miles per hour on a one-way run, and became the fastest automobile driver in history. However, to establish a recognized world record, a driver is required to make the drive on a two-way run. Cobb, therefore, still holds the official world record despite Thompson's run.

An interesting thing about Thompson's feats is that his car cost less than one-half that of Cobb's.

A measured mile is laid out in the center of a 13-mile course, and on it new designs are pitted against time. Picture a car near the starting point. The man with the green flag gives the starting signal, and the car roars toward the finish line. An electronic timer records finish time on paper tape as the car passes through the light beams known as "traps."

Five men with telephones are stationed along the course. These men climb ladders to watch over a large area for any trouble which needs reporting. In case of

accident, they speed a waiting ambulance to the spot.
Careful pre-run check for mechanical condition, rigid operating rules, and helmets and goggles keep accident rates low, with little likelihood of death. In spite of the fact that Bonneville is the world's safest place for racing, NHRA rules prohibit the participation of any driver who is under twenty-one years of age without a notarized consent from parents or guardian.

A week of speed at Bonneville is the highlight of the NHRA speed trials. The top three NHRA races are Cado Mills, Texas; Akron, Ohio; and Madera, California. Another organization, the Automobile Timing Association of America, held its First Annual World Series of Drag Racing at Lawrenceville Airport in Illinois on October 2 and 3, 1954. This organization was formed recently to stimulate hot-rodding in the Middle West.

Hot-rod builders and racers are estimated at two hundred thousand, while the number of participants in the sport reaches two million.

Hot-rodding is strictly an amateur sport; there are no prizes of money. Drivers race for trophies and glory, but none make a living from their winnings.

This is not the case in stock-car racing. Stock cars are regular passenger cars that can be bought in an automobile salesroom. The only changes which can be made on them for stock-car racing are a number of things which promote safety at high speeds, and motor parts changes listed by the manufacturers and available to the general public. Rules are under the control of the National Association for Stock Car Automobile Racing. This is the largest racing group in the world if size is based on the number of races run, and its initials, NASCAR, hold meaning for many people.

Earning a living as a daredevil driver is a rugged existence. For NASCAR racers, the season begins in Florida, where Speed Week events at Daytona Beach draw about twenty to thirty thousand spectators. This roaring week of speed is not confined to stock cars. Cars of every description sweep across the sands breaking records, thrilling the spectators, winning prize money or disappointment for their drivers. Sometimes death is the winner, for in spite of safety precautions, automobile racing is a dangerous game.

During the year, some stock-car drivers follow the trail from border to border, piling up points and prizes in the rugged races which follow. Some drive from one fairground to another at night, snatch some sleep in their cars, tune up and head for the starting line in one or more races during the day.

Two of the big NASCAR races are the "Southern 500," held at Darlington, South Carolina, and the Carnival of Speed at the Memphis-Arkansas Speedway in Tennessee. Here winners collect high points and big prize money.

Some of the winner's money goes to his pit crew, some for replacement parts on his machine and for repair bills. A stock-car race driver not only puts up with a hard life away from home while he is racing, but his job offers no security for the future, if he lives to have one.

In spite of these undesirable aspects, men continue to roar down dusty, hot race tracks.

Much has been done to protect the drivers in stock-car races so that there are few deaths and injuries in NASCAR-sanctioned races. In addition to the required crash helmets which drivers must wear, quick-release safety belts must be fastened to the frames of the cars. Crash bars replace bumpers; the top and frame of the car must be heavily braced. Doors must be securely fastened. Before any action can take place, a doctor, ambulance, and fire-fighting equipment must be present.

There are safety rules to protect spectators, too. For instance, all NASCAR-sanctioned tracks must provide a heavy guard rail which is usually reinforced with steel.

Safety is a major concern of the United States Auto Club which supervises major auto races throughout the United States. Its activities include many performance tests, the Indianapolis 500 mile race, the Pike's Peak Hill

Climb, professional sports car racing, and other speed and endurance runs. This organization has taken over much of the function of the Contest Board of the American Automobile Association which severed all connections with automobile racing in 1955 because of the high accident rate and insurance problems.

Although many of the factors which go into the making of the cars of the future are developed and tested on the speedways, there is a great question as to whether or not what is gained makes it worth the tragic deaths which haunt the racing trail. And can watching automobiles at high speed be considered a sport when it costs so much in human lives?

In spite of the dangers, some adventurous men continue to risk their lives for the thrill of the race, fame, and the prizes offered to the winners. In addition to stock-car racing, men compete at high speed in sports cars and professional racing cars, some of which are called Grand Prix cars.

Classification of racing cars and sports cars is a bewildering problem to many spectators. Even authorities find it difficult to define a sports car. Many more European sports cars are seen on the road today, but not all European cars qualify as sports cars. Generally speaking, a sports car is one built for the sheer sport of driving. It doubles as a means of transportation and as a racing car. Careful engineering features enable it to compete in the most difficult road races. Two seats, the ability to hug a curve at high speeds without turning over, fast pickup and good brakes are a few of the characteristics. Most are open cars, but some are convertibles, and a relatively few have hard tops. Equipment includes standard headlights, self-starters, spare tires, and certain tools. Engineering features alone outlaw many of the cars which Americans call sports cars, but the cars built in the United States and driven by the millionaire sportsman Briggs Cunningham can perform with the best that Europe has to offer.

In the United States, road racing has met with numerous problems, including the withdrawal of Air Force bases as racing grounds, but the Sports Car Club of America strives to increase public interest. They serve the increasing number of amateurs who enjoy the skill and fun of driving for its own sake. Thousands of sports-car fans gather annually for road races on courses temporarily blocked off from other traffic for such famous races as Watkins Glen, New York; Pebble Beach, California; Elkhart Lake, Wisconsin; and Sebring, Florida, and at numerous other places including any available abandoned airstrip. They participate in hill climbs in which cars climb one at a time up steep slopes. They engage in rallies, sporting events in which sports-car owners pit themselves against preestablished times for covering a given course.

One of the most important sports-car races in the United States is the annual Florida International Twelve-hour Grand Prix of Endurance. At Sebring, Florida, cars roar over a flat, fast course which is 5.2 miles of short straightaways, switchbacks, and unbanked turns until the checkered flag falls twelve hours after the starting flag. The man who has covered the most laps takes the grand prize, but there is a winner in each class. This race of endurance is run under rules of the great European road race, Le Mans, and is the only one in the United States which contributes points to the international program.

In Europe, road racing is a much more popular sport than in the United States. High-priced professionals drive for European car manufacturers who take great pride in the performance of their cars on the rugged courses. They drive sport and racing cars which are special versions of regular passenger cars to gain prestige for their manufacturers and to boost sales.

The Le Mans sports-car race is considered by many racing enthusiasts as one of the greatest races in the world. In this twenty-four-hour race, the faster you drive, the more miles you cover. The same driver does not race twice around the clock, but must rest at intervals while another drives for him.

Suppose you are driving in a European road race such

as Le Mans. You might be driving a fire-engine-red Ferrari or a Maserati or an Alfa-Romeo representing Italy, a Cunningham painted blue and white in the international racing colors of the United States, a silver Mercedes Benz for Germany, a bottle-green Jaguar or Bentley for England, a blue Gordini for France, or any one of the many beautiful, sleek, and able sports cars that are lined up at the starting line.

Before the start for which Le Mans is so famous, you look nervously at the cars lined up near the pits, pointing out at 45-degree angles as though angle-parked. Each car has been carefully checked and rechecked to make certain that the proper tools and spare parts are in place, that the engine and mechanical parts are in top condition, and that the fuel tank is topped and sealed. No car may use any repair parts other than those carried aboard, with the exception of wheels and tires. No car may refuel or stop for oil or water until it has gone about 230 miles, or 28 laps.

You have carefully warmed your engine, shut it off, and put the key in place. The gearshift lever is already in low, and your safety belt is carefully laid open so that you can fasten it quickly.

Now the warning signal is given, and seconds later the green flag drops. Some walk briskly to their cars, others run. You try to keep calm as you fasten your belt, let out the clutch, and push the starter. Off you go with the pack roaring down the road, enjoying the feel of the wind, the music of the engine, and the smell of the exhaust. You feel close to your car, almost a part of it as it leaps forward. Again and again you cover the circuit of 8.38 miles of roads, taking severe corners as fast as possible but slowly enough for safety. You have learned all the tricks of driving on the course, and you know exactly where to brake at each corner. You know your car's capabilities, and you stay within them, driving as slowly as you dare without losing the lead.

When the sun goes down, you are still driving round and round the course over the rolling French countryside. There has been time out for changing drivers and for minor repairs in the pit, but many of the cars have suffered far more than minor injuries during this long grind at high speed which overheats engines, shatters gearboxes, blows tires, crumbles axles, burns out brakes. In the 1955 race, death and destruction dominated the scene after a Mercedes crashed into the back of an Austin-Healey. Flaming debris which killed spectators made this the worst race-track tragedy on record.

Another famous race is the annual Pan-American Road

Soap Boxes, Hot Rods, and Racing Cars

Race. Here drivers of many classes of cars race against death for gold and glory. Sometimes it seems that death is the winner. As cars speed northward toward the United States border, they twist and turn, up and down mountain grades, past the rim of a volcano, over newly paved sections of road, and over gravel. In contrast to the closed circuits where drivers repeat the same problems, each situation is new to the driver of the Carrera Panamericana.

Cars roar ahead day after day for about five days, stopping at night so that drivers can rest and eat and mechanics can work on the cars. Race time is fiesta time in Mexico, but gay times have ended in disaster when spectators have been hurled to their death by the cars which race along at terrific speeds over the 1,900-mile course. Here tragedy and speed go together in spite of great efforts to make the race a safer one.

The Mille Miglia is another of the world's most famous races. Imagine the strain of averaging 79 miles per hour on a thousand miles of roads that twist through mountains and towns in Italy. Fast and slow cars begin this race at such intervals that the pack comes to the finish line at nearly the same time. All of Italy feels the excitement of race day with as many as 20 million persons watching along the route. The rest of Italy listens to the progress of their favorite drivers by radio.

The Nurburg Ring is 14 miles of winding road in the Eifel Mountains of Germany with about 180 curves. The Tourist Trophy is a 7-mile circuit around the top of a mountain in Ireland. These are among the races which are included in the world's championships for sports cars.

Races with Grand Prix cars are popular in Europe, too. A Grand Prix car is a car built just for racing and is limited only by engine capacity. It is somewhat like an Indianapolis race car in appearance but is built for the right and left turns of road racing on the many kinds of road surfaces in the series of races ruled by the Fédération Internationale de l'Automobile (FIA). Even though there are many Grand Prix races throughout Europe, only one race in the United States contributes points toward the world championship. This is the Indianapolis 500, held on a track which is affectionately called the Brickyard.

To many racing enthusiasts, the oval track at Indianapolis does not provide the interest afforded by the curves and hills of road racing. A different kind of skill is required, but skill and courage are musts in both kinds of racing. American racing cars are different, too. Since they need to make only left-hand turns, they are built to turn left at high speeds but not right. American racing cars do not need powerful brakes, since drivers slow down for curves with less pressure on the accelerators. American racing cars could not compete in European road races, but they are the best in the world for the track racing for which they are built.

Race day, May 30, is typically American, with parades of brass bands, majorettes, balloons before the race, and tired people who have sat up all night for a good view. Pit men check their tools and stand in readiness to make fast repairs, change four tires and refuel their cars. Cameras click and tension mounts as the strains of "Back Home in Indiana" fill the air. Then come the classic words: "Gentlemen, start your engines." Two minutes later the pace car moves in front with the first row of qualifiers behind it. The pace car moves into the pits and the green flag drops. They are off for the long grind, each one hoping to win America's most famous race.

Sometimes the yellow flags and caution lights tell of tragedy, as in the 1955 race when the hurtling cars slowed down until Bill Vukovich, two-time winner of the big race, was carried from the speedway after a fatal accident. Soon the race continued at its dizzy pace, and spectators were once more thrilling to the speed of fast cars.

Drama, triumph, and tragedy follow the racing trail. Racing men are a strange breed who are devoted to their sport. Although some may race for the prize money, many, including millionaires, are in the game for the sport of it, for the love of driving fast and driving well. Only the best win a place in auto racing's Hall of Fame in Dearborn, Michigan.

Obviously there is far more to automobile racing than stepping hard on the accelerator and just letting the car travel as fast as it will toward the finish line. There is an art to taking a corner at exactly the right speed for safety but at the same time one that is fast enough to win the race. There is skill in making the most of every bend and twist in the road. There is possible danger to even the best from trouble that is beyond his control. The world of racing drivers is one of skill and daring.

The world of automobiles benefits in many ways from the knowledge gained from automobile racing, including better tires, steering, improved fuel and engines, better metals, and safer cars. The many tragedies, and especially the accident of Le Mans in 1955 that killed eighty-two persons, have made it evident that stricter safety rules are needed in many events to protect both drivers and spectators. Some think that the dangerous sport of automobile racing should be outlawed. Certainly, there are many sports which contribute more to physical fitness. Not only do drivers endanger their lives, but spectators miss the healthful benefits of exercise which come to those who participate in many other sports where speed is king.

BOATS IN THE PARK

COLORFUL FLAGS announce a boat regatta which will bring thousands of visitors to the city. Outstanding crews will row on the river the first day, and during the remainder of race week model power boats and model sailing yachts will compete on ponds and lakes throughout the park.

You take your place among the several thousand crew enthusiasts who line the shore of the river for the rowing regatta of the local amateur rowing clubs. Cabin cruisers and craft of every description which have gathered near the finish line afford a fine view for those aboard.

The 2,000-meter (1¼-mile) straightaway has been carefully measured, and six parallel 50-foot lanes are ready for the boats that will glide their length at full speed. Flag buoys mark the course every quarter mile for the entire length, from the starting sign to the finish. Two motorboats patrol the area to prevent other boats from entering the course or from disturbing the smooth water.

Six eight-oared shells are in position, with the sterns of their boats at the starting line. Each bowman wears a colored cap which designates the lane to which his shell has been assigned. Each boat must keep in its own water throughout the race.

Everyone is tense as the first command, "Get ready," comes from the starter. "Ready all," he says as he looks about to make certain that all crews are ready, and then shouts, "Row!" through his megaphone.

The shells quiver and leap ahead as the eight men in each boat move in perfect rhythm and grace. Each shell lifts and slips silently forward along her course. The constant rumbling of the sliding seats, the yells of the coxswains, the clicking of the oars as they turn into the locks, and the swish of the water are drowned out by the chatter of the spectators.

Many who watch know little about the simple points of rowing. They are here to see one crew of well-trained oarsmen surpass the others. To them the announcer seems to be speaking in an almost foreign language; but to you, who have learned some of the strange vocabulary of crew competitions, the race is more interesting.

The announcer says, "There is beautiful spacing with a fine run between the strokes." You know that "spacing" is the distance between successive sets of strokes. "Run"

Boats in the Park

AN EIGHT-OARED SHELL

means the speed at which the boat travels between strokes. "Feathering" is the turning of the blade as it is lifted from the water to reduce wind resistance. When the announcer commends the coordination at the catch and the recovery, you know "catch" as the point at which the blades drop into the water and "recovery" as that at which the oar finishes the "pull through" and is brought back, feathered, to the catch position. This is accomplished by the oarsman sliding forward on the rolling seat, arms outstretched, controlling the slide speed by the shoes fixed in permanent position on the keel of the shell. One man fails to clear the water when he should, so the announcer says the man has "caught a crab."

Now the crowd breaks into spontaneous cheers as the underdog sweeps past the others and breaks into the lead at the halfway mark. Muscles, lungs, and hearts are straining, but you have learned to watch oars rather than men. You can judge the speed of a boat by watching the swirls or whirlpools which are made when the oars leave the water. If the blade of number 7 clears or matches the whirlpools on his side when the men are rowing 37 strokes per minute, they are showing good form and speed.

To count the strokes per minute, you begin the count as the oarsmen start at the stern end of their slides, with their bodies nearly between their knees and their blades dropping into the water. You count a full stroke, from catch to catch, for a minute. Most races are rowed at a rate of 32 to 40 strokes per minute.

The "stroke" on each boat, the man who sits in the number-8 position from the bow, is calling for that extra burst of speed which may bring his crew to the front. He sets the pace for a perfectly coordinated crew where each man must show excellent powers of concentration, endurance, and determination. Each one needs a fine sense of rhythm and ability to work in perfect harmony with the man ahead.

Sometimes the work of the coxswain is the factor which determines the winner. In addition to knowing how to steer, he must learn to take advantage of the winds and tides and watch constantly for faults during training. He gives the necessary commands and keeps the crew informed of the position of the other boats in the race. Today, an outstanding coxswain and the perfect coordination of the crew bring an unfavored shell across the finish line a full length before a more favored crew. Cheers pour forth from the spectators who line the shore and watch from boats at the edge of the river. When the winners return to the boathouse, the coxswain will be tossed into the water in traditional style.

Some of the races which follow are included in the seventeen events of a National Regatta. There are single

Boats in the Park

sculls, in which one man rows a light racing craft with an oar in each hand. Long oars called sweeps are used individually by oarsmen in certain races. There are double sculls, four-oared shells with coxswain, four-oared shells without coxswain, and a number of others. Each event brings the thrills of a race in which men exhibit the results of good training and sportsmanship.

Your program tells of a schoolboy regatta. Perhaps your school is interested in rowing and wants to form a team which can compete in schoolboy regattas. There are a number of difficulties, but a large number of boys have managed to begin the wonderful sport of rowing while in secondary school. First, there must be a river or body of water on which to row. Second, there must be equipment or money to buy it. Perhaps your school will be able to allot the money if enough boys show a sincere interest. Contact local rowing clubs to see if they can help you start a schoolboy team.

Intercollegiate rowing events such as the famous Harvard-Yale classic and the regattas of the Intercollegiate Rowing Association are discussed in the program. It also describes the most famous regatta in the world, the English Henley, which features the well-known race for single scullers known as the Diamond Sculls. More than a hundred races have been run, and on each occasion thousands and thousands of people line the shores of the Thames River no matter what the weather. Even heavy snowstorms have failed to stop the big event, but sometimes races must be rerun because of rough water. One year, the winners waded ashore when their boat, after finishing the race, sank near the shore. Year after year, the English Henley stirs the sporting blood of the country and causes excitement far and wide.

Other competitions among amateur boat clubs are listed on your program, but for many local sportsmen the most interesting announcement is that of the model boat races which begin tomorrow.

A green flag flies in the park, with white letters that read I.M.P.B.A. A crowd has gathered around the edge of the lake to watch the time trials of the International Model Power Boat Association. Contestants who have brought their models from cities far and near stand behind the judges, making last-minute adjustments with loving care.

In the center of the lake a man in waterproof trousers and boots called "waders" controls the center stick to which a strong wire is fastened. Another man in waders is preparing to start the motor of his model, which is fastened to the other end of the guide wire. Suddenly the noise is terrific and the boat is hard to hold. With a firm hand, the owner places the boat in the water with a forward push, and it is off. Faster and faster it whirs around a circle 105 feet in diameter, held on its course by the wire which is attached to the center pole. When the boat skips out of the water, some of the spectators are splashed by the water. Now the timers are counting the laps and measuring the speed. During four laps the boat traveled a quarter of a mile and it did so at a speed equivalent to 72 miles per hour. The noise stops, for the gasoline supply has been exhausted. Smoke rises above the water as the hot engine sinks into it at the end of the race.

Another boat is fastened to the wire and it skims around the circle. One after another, little outboards and inboards race before the judges until as many as thirty-two have competed in various classes in one day.

At the end of the competitions, trophies which have been supplied by the local club are presented to the winners. The owners of the models dream about and plan for the next model power boat races.

The exact time of the next event depends largely on the weather, for model yachts without motors cannot race when the air is still.

For many years, midget-yacht enthusiasts have been

testing and racing their highly tuned craft on their clubs' sailing waters. Throughout the United States, about fifty ponds have been built especially for model yacht races with walks along the sides and ends. But the races scheduled for tomorrow will be held on a pond in the park where men, women, boys, and girls will wear waders to start their boats and retrieve them at the end of a heat. These people are the skippers and the mates of the yachts. A heat is a race from one end of the pool to the other. When every yacht has raced every other yacht once, a round of racing has been completed.

The day brings bright sunshine and a brisk wind. Members of the local model-yachting club and those who come from a distance carefully transport their precious models to the park. These boats are more than toys. They are carefully designed for high speed and built of fine materials such as cedar, mahogany, plastic, or Fiberglas. Stainless-steel fishing leader is generally used for the mast rigging. On deck, there is a complicated arrangement for adjusting the sails. A device mounted on the stern deck of each yacht is called a vane. This steers the yacht on the course chosen by the skipper. Vanes are operated by the wind and use a light balsa-wood "feather" to catch it. These devices actually steer a yacht better than many a helmsman could.

Boats range in size from 24 inches to 76 inches, but the most popular class, Class M (Marblehead), is 50 inches over-all, with 800 square inches of sail. Boats are rated for various classes according to a set of rules of the Model Yacht Racing Association of America so that competing skippers have an equal chance of winning. One class does not race against another class, but clubs from different regions compete in scheduled races for various classes.

Today's race is one for boats in Class M. The owners are standing at the starting line making last-second adjustments before the start of the race. No crew can help after the race has begun. The skipper can't trim sails after the starting gun, so he must decide now what sail and vane settings will give the yacht the best speed for the course.

At the starting signal the boats are away toward the other end of the 800-foot pool, working their way against the wind. One touches the side of the pool. The skipper puts the yacht on the opposite tack and releases it so that it can continue up the pond.

The yachts have reached the finish line and their skippers are taking them from the water to prepare for the run down the pool with the wind. When this heat is over, they will plan for the next race with different yachts.

Boys, girls, and adults thrill to the beauty and rivalry of the race. At lunch time, the skipper of a radio-controlled sailing yacht demonstrates his complete control over the boat as he sails it through an obstacle course and puts the yacht through intricate figures by pushing a button. He uses his battery-operated radio transmitter to haul in the sails and let them out.

As the regatta in the park comes to an end with the awarding of trophies, you look forward to more sailing, to participating in events for juniors during race week at your own yacht club.

SAILS AT FULL SPEED

JUNIOR RACE DAY is an exciting one for everyone at the yacht club. Before anyone can race, he must meet the requirements for graduation from the sailing course. Members range in age from eight to seventeen years, but before anyone can set foot in a boat without donning his life preserver he must pass a swimming test. Safety is the watchword of junior yacht clubs and of experts alike.

Ground instruction comes before actual experience in boats, but this kind of summer school is extremely popular. In addition to learning how to handle a boat in the water, junior sailors are taught land duties of keeping a boat in shape. Many who would grumble about painting, scraping, and sanding the back porch work on their boats for long hours with loving care. For those who know and love boats, caring for them is seldom a chore.

You will graduate from a rating of "seaman" to "mate" and on to "skipper" as you fulfill the detailed list of requirements, but it's all wonderful fun. The most exciting part of the program of a junior yacht club is learning how to race. Graduates compete among their own group at first, but when two clubs race against each other, the spirit is high.

Today your club is host to a neighboring one. Eighteen 12-foot sneak boxes, boats which look like the one in the picture, will sail over a 3-mile course. Each skipper has drawn a number from a hat to determine which of the boats will be his for the race.

Each one has checked his boat long before the ten-minute warning gun. Now stop watches are set as the three-minute gun sends the boats into position for the start. The right approach to the starting line can make a big difference in the success of a boat in a race, so sailors guide their boats with care, jockeying as they try to get into the best position before the next gun.

The starter calls the seconds. Four . . . three . . . two . . . one. A black ball drops and the starting gun goes off, giving a visual and auditory signal that the race has begun. The boats cross the imaginary line between the yacht club and a floating barrel which acts as a marker.

Together the boats sail the first leg of the course, round another barrel marker, and begin the second leg of the triangular course. Now it's anybody's race.

As they begin the last leg, the breeze improves, and a few boats manage to break in front of the crowd. One from your team and one from the other are reaching the finish line in close order.

The gun announces a winner and the cheers from the spectators tell you that someone on your team has won this race. This means that the trophy will stay at your club. The winner and his crew will receive a prize such as a compass, a flashlight, or something which can be used on the boat. And the whole group will feast on sandwiches and ice cream while they discuss the race.

In future summers, a few of these sailors may be chosen to compete in the National Sears Cup Junior Championship which brings together the top sailors in the country under eighteen years of age. Usually this series of races is held on the Atlantic Coast, but clubs from other parts of the United States and Canada compete to determine the North American Junior Champion.

Most of the boys and girls who sail continue to enjoy their sport for many years. Some will sail year after year because of the beauty and the benefits they enjoy from fresh air, sunshine, and good sportsmanship. Many will continue to compete with other sailors in some of the thousands of races which are held on the many waterways in and around the nation.

The sport of sailing is growing rapidly in popularity among people of all ages. Sailboat estimates have reached the half-million mark, with fleets of small boats sailing on many lakes and rivers which were not used for boating before. One of the reasons for the increased number of boats is the availability of boat kits and the willingness of owners to make and repair boats themselves. This cuts the cost of purchasing and upkeep, so that today anyone within easy reach of a body of water can become a sailor of a small boat if he has one hundred dollars and the will, time, and ability to work. More money, time, and work are needed to keep a boat trim and to store it if you live in an area where this is necessary. Many boats cost thousands of dollars.

If you want to learn to sail, join a class at a yacht club if there is one nearby. If there is none, perhaps an experienced sailor may be willing to show you how to handle a boat. Study a beginner's book of sailing to learn the names of parts of a boat and their uses. Your librarian may be able to help you find such a book.

No matter what kind of a boat you choose, when you become an expert sailor you can enjoy the thrill of a race. At most regattas, boats are classed for racing according to their design. Some of the major classes are pictured on page 86. If boats of various classes race, handicaps are used to make the competition a fair one.

An unusual type of race is a "one-of-a-kind," in which a number of classes race to see which is the fastest boat and to give new designs a chance to test their speed against the classic ones.

Throughout the country thousands of regattas are held each year, but two of the most famous race weeks are held at Larchmont, on Long Island Sound, and at Marblehead, Massachusetts. At these, races are held by classes, each boat racing against other boats of the same design and size, with about thirty different classes of boats taking part. On some days more than four hundred different craft race over triangular courses, with the length of the race depending on the weather. Spectators and participants come from far and near for the fun and the beauty of white sails on the blue water.

Young yachtsmen sometimes compete with men of all ages in senior racing events. In the second annual race of North American Sailing Championship, an eighteen-year-old skipper named Gene Wallet III outdistanced the best sailors in the country. At the age of nineteen, Wallet and his crew repeated their success, and once again Wallet was winner of the Mallory Cup and the title of "best sailor in the United States and Canada."

SLOOP

YAWL

Some Common Rigs For Yachts That You Can Easily Identify

CAT-BOAT

SCHOONER

KETCH

Even the losers in this series of races were winners of countless elimination races and expert sailors in all kinds of weather.

Some serious sailors bundle up in warm clothing and race in small boats on numerous weekends all through the cold of winter. They claim that this helps them to improve their sailing tactics for summer racing and the exercise keeps them fit.

Racing in small boats provides action in winter and in summer, and many prefer them to the larger yachts which race long distances over the ocean.

Ocean racing is a more expensive sport but one that is a beautiful spectacle to those who watch and those who compete. You can fly to Bermuda in comfort in a few hours from Newport, Rhode Island, but there are yachtsmen who prefer to get there the hard way. Every two years a fleet of seaworthy sailboats travel through 635 miles of ocean in a test of speed, stamina, and racing skill, to reach Bermuda after more than a hundred hours of work on the part of the men who love ocean racing.

From Saint Petersburg to Havana, from Miami to Nassau, from San Diego to Acapulco, and over the 2,200-mile course from California to Honolulu, able sailors race their beautiful boats.

The most famous of ocean races is the Fastnet Race, 600 miles around Fastnet rock on the southern coast of Ireland, ending at Plymouth, England.

Today the number of ocean yachts is small compared

with the many small boats which are becoming so popular. More and more people are enjoying the fresh air and sunshine, and the thrill of a race in the safety of sails at full speed.

FASTEST BOATS AFLOAT

THE BOOM of the starting gun sends powerboats streaking over waterways throughout the country. The number of these boats has increased tremendously in the past few years and motor boat racing has become a popular recreation for their drivers and spectators.

Many kinds of motorboats roar for the finish line. They are classed according to motor and hull. Outboards, the most common variety, have motors which are clamped on the stern of the boats. When motors are built inside the hull, the boats are called inboards. These boats achieve greater speeds than the outboards, because of greater horsepower, but they are more expensive to build, and they are more cumbersome to trail from one regatta site to another.

Boats differ in hull construction, too. The hull of a hydroplane is built so that at high speeds it lifts itself partly out of the water and the boat skims along with less resistance from the water than received by other craft.

Many who race outboards soup up the motors with great care, spending weeks in a machine shop working with delicate precision. After much testing, they enter boats in races which last about five minutes each. And win or lose, they return to the job of tinkering with the motors in preparation for the next regatta. This class of boats is called *racing hydroplanes*.

The runabout is a boat intended to be a family craft but now used for racing, too. These boats are more seaworthy than hydroplanes, but since they ride *through* the water, they are not as fast.

Cruisers are powerboats equipped with cabin, plumbing, and all the arrangements necessary for living aboard. A new type of racing, predicted-log contests with cabin cruisers, is becoming very popular. These first-class sporting events are extremely safe and provide many thrills. In such a contest, each skipper, running at any predetermined speed which he selects, predicts the time at which he must start and pass each control point in order to finish at a designated time. His score is determined by the difference between his actual time and the predicted time.

One of the features which makes predicted-log contests so exciting is the absence of any timepiece after the boat has crossed the starting line. The only one on the boat who knows the time of day is the official observer who travels with the crew to make observations for the race committee. He records the passing of control points and the finish time. He is the only one who knows how the contest is progressing, and he is not permitted to tell the others.

If all predicted logs were correct and all boats in the contest were traveling in perfect time, they would all reach the finish line at the same time. Imagine nearing the end of such a contest with some boats behind you, others ahead, and no knowledge of which are too slow and which are too fast. The observer just grins when he is asked for information.

When the scores are checked, approved, and posted, captains and crews gather eagerly to compare results. Only when the last score has been posted can those with a small percentage of error know whether or not their hopes of winning have been fulfilled. And those who don't win this race are always ready to try again in a sport which combines fun and safety and increases boating skill.

Racing with stock outboards began in 1949. These are boats with motors that have not been changed after factory purchase. Although the fastest boats are those with racing motors, stock outboard racing is extremely popular.

Each year several hundred sanctioned regattas are held in the United States, in which there are races for numerous classes of boats. Drivers of the boats vary greatly in age, with one class for racing drivers between the ages of nine and fifteen.

The National Outboard Association, an organization formed in 1950, sanctions races and considers their winners official champions. Another organization, the American Power Boat Association, is considered the authority by many. It governs races over a larger area of the United States, sanctions all types of motorboat competitions, and is the one recognized as the official United States representative by the Union of International Motorboating.

Since outboard motorboating has grown like Topsy in the last few years, there are many members in both organizations. About 4,500 racing members pay dues to the American Power Boat Association each year, and approximately half of these race stock outboards.

One of the many popular outboard events is the annual Winnebagoland Marathon in Wisconsin. You might be one of 100,000 people who have come from many distances to watch more than 200 outboards whiz along the 92-mile course. The drivers vary in age from fourteen to sixty, with boys and girls doing some of the fastest times.

In the stirring seconds before the race, drivers in the usual helmets and life jackets jockey for positions which will bring them to the starting line just as the gun opens the race. Being over the starting line before the signal disqualifies a driver immediately.

From the roaring start to the end of the race, planes

circle overhead to keep a constant check on the contestants and report any trouble to headquarters. A public-address system speeds ground workers of the Coast Guard and various civic organizations to the rescue of any drivers who encounter accidents. An extensive safety program helps to make this race a popular one, for just as danger increases with speed in automobile racing, so it does in boating.

After you have watched various groups of boats thunder across the starting line, the crowd waits for news of their favorites. Announcers send information over the public-address system telling of the progress which is being made.

Excitement is high again when the boats flash toward the finish line. The checkered flag falls, and cheers and applause burst forth.

After each race there is rigid inspection by officials of the American Power Boat Association to make certain that the motors have not been altered. Any which have been souped up can no longer qualify as stock models and cannot be counted as winners. Prizes are awarded to many, and all who finish receive bronze medallions in recognition of their completion of the long, rugged course.

One of the winners of the marathon at Winnebagoland was a fourteen-year-old boy who had earned money to buy materials to build his boat by caddying and mowing lawns the summer before. He and his father made the boat together. They are just one example of the many families who have fun together with boats.

It is estimated that twenty million persons enjoyed the sport of boating in one year. Only a small percentage of these raced their boats, but the number who did is large and growing larger.

With racing hydroplanes blazing over the waterways at speeds over 100 miles an hour, and with increased traffic due to the spectacular rise in popularity of boating, safety regulations must be strictly enforced. The safety committee plays an important part during regatta time and all during the boating season in reducing the accident record. Although some drivers are lucky enough to remain unhurt after being thrown from flying speedboats, some have been seriously injured when flipped from boats at high speed.

Another sport which is growing in popularity is water skiing, a sport which looks more dangerous and difficult than it really is. Beginners as well as experts can thrill to the swift motion of their skis as they skim over the water behind a fast boat. This is one of the reasons why water skiing is such a fast-growing sport. This hazardous-looking sport can be conquered by young as well as old with little danger of accident when the skier uses proper equipment and has competent instruction. Grandparents and grandchildren can learn together and even compete in the game of water skiing. Needless to say, all water skiers must be swimmers, but if they can swim, they can ski.

Water skiing is a branch of show business, a resort attraction, and a competitive game. The tournaments

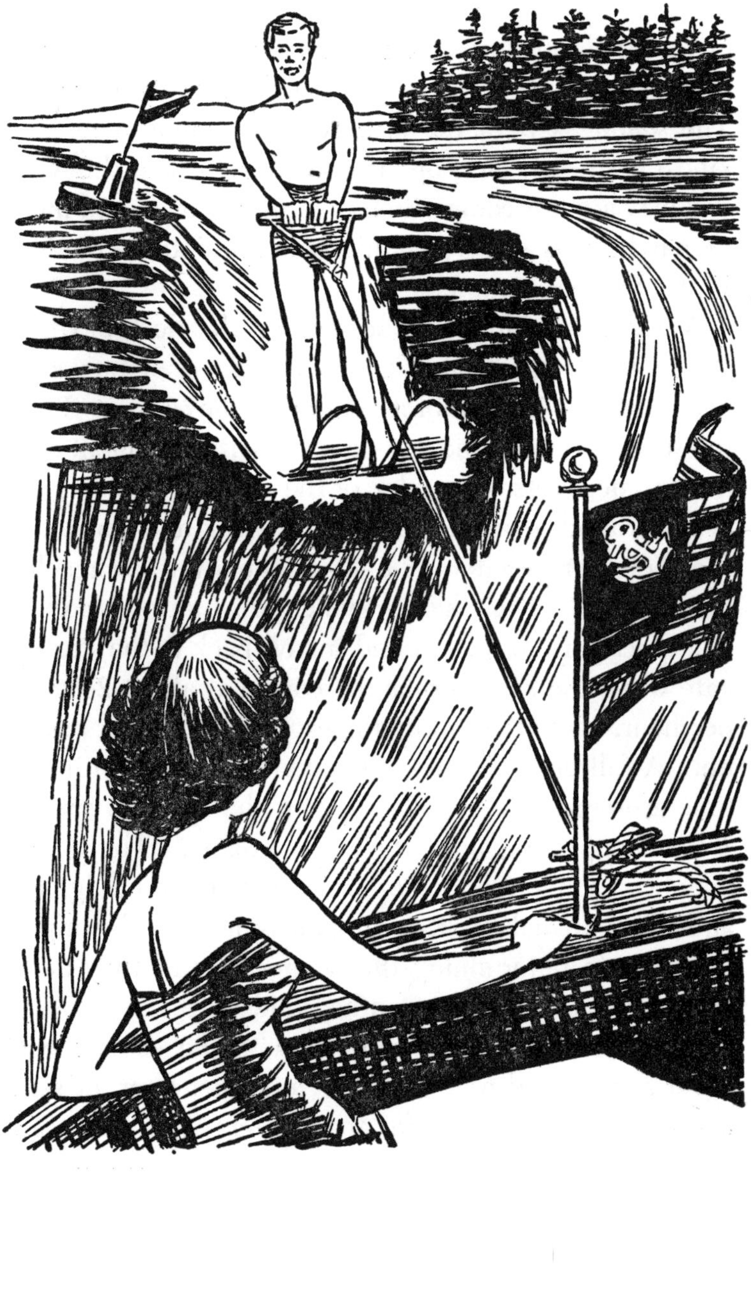

are divided into three classes: trick riding, jumping, and *slalom*. Only the last is concerned mainly with speed. The *slalom* is both the fastest and the most strenuous kind of water skiing, but if you plan to race this way, you may aim for competition in local, national, and international levels under the sponsorship of the American Water Ski Association.

A water-ski *slalom* is a race against the clock in which the skier zigzags around a series of floats or buoys set in the water. Then another skier runs the course. From the starting gate to the end gate there is excitement each time a skier crosses the edge of the wake of the boat and skims around a buoy. He weaves back and forth at a speed of approximately 22 miles per hour until he reaches the end gate. Then the boat which pulls him loops around in a quick turn to the left and travels back to the starting gate while the skier reruns the course at about 24 miles per hour. Points are lost for each buoy that is passed up. A fall ends the run, but points acquired until that time are credited. In case of ties, the speed is successively stepped up until the tie is broken. The course may be run on either one or two skis, but good judgment and ability to make split-second decisions play the important part in determining the winner, just as they do in snow *slaloms* and in many other kinds of racing.

Whether you aim to compete with the experts who cover a measured mile about 50 miles per hour, or skim over water on skis just for the excitement of the com-

Fastest Boats Afloat

bination of speed, sun, spray, and water, water skiing can be fun.

Neighborhood groups who share the expense of the boat and outboard motors necessary for this sport, as well as skiing schools, are bringing the sport within the reach of more people. If you live near water and belong to a family who can spend seven hundred dollars or more for an outboard runabout and motor, and more for its upkeep, or if you live near a water-ski school where equipment is supplied, you may become an experienced water skier in a few months.

Competing in a big regatta with the fastest inboards is a much more expensive kind of boating. An inboard hydroplane in the unlimited class might easily cost fifty thousand dollars.

The Orange Bowl Regatta in Florida is a famous one which draws boats of a wide price range from a variety of countries. Here the International Grand Prix climaxes a number of days of racing of many classes of boats.

The Silver Cup is competed for each year in a race staged by the Detroit Yacht Club. On the Detroit River where giants of the speedboat world battle each year, there is fierce rivalry and breath-taking excitement.

Another coveted award is the President's Trophy which is presented each year by the President of the United States to the winner of the famous race on the Potomac River at the nation's capital. This racing event began in 1926 when President Coolidge was in office.

Powerboat racing's most sought-after prize is the American Power Boat Association Gold Cup. This trophy was first presented in 1904 to a boat that averaged 23.6 miles per hour. Today, average speeds near 100 miles per hour take the prize. For many years the Gold Cup stayed in Detroit, Michigan, where rich men and women spent vast sums of money and where mechanics worked long hours to produce boats that were the fastest in the United States. Detroit was the speedboat capital until suddenly, in the summer of 1950, an ultramodern boat called Slo-Mo-Shun IV appeared in Seattle, Washington. On June 26, 1950, Stanley S. Sayres drove his boat, Slo-Mo-Shun IV, on Lake Washington over a one-mile course and back again. She went streaking down the course at a terrific pace, with great white spurts of spray shooting up as high as 30 feet to form a roosterlike tail of water in the wake of the boat. Official timers clocked the speed at 160.323 miles per hour. This was a new world's record! This was the fastest boat in the world, a boat

Fastest Boats Afloat

which has since broken its own record by traveling a mile in less than 20 seconds, or 178.497 miles per hour.

Slo-Mo-Shun IV, with its now-famous roosterlike tail of water, caused great excitement in 1950 in Detroit, where it won the treasured Gold Cup when driver Ted Jones averaged the almost unbelievable speed of 78.216 miles per hour for the 90-mile race.

A week later, throngs of people jammed the shores of the Detroit River for the Harmsworth. From 1920 to 1933, world-famous Gar Wood completely dominated the international competition for the Harmsworth Trophy with his "Miss America." In the 1950 Harmsworth, Slo-Mo-Shun IV was driven by Lou Fageol through the 80-mile course at a total average speed of 95.903 miles per hour. Again, the boat had set a new record.

This was just the beginning of success for boatowner Stanley Sayres. The race brought him the honor of being the first person to win the Gold Cup five consecutive times.

In summer, 1959, Donald Campbell of England broke his own 1957 record of 239.07 miles per hour for jet-driven speed boats when he traveled at 260.35 miles per hour. Sometime before this, two men were killed when their boats disintegrated at speeds of about 200 miles per hour. Campbell's boat was built twice as strong as a jet airplane. Campbell's father is the only man ever to hold both the car and boat world speed records.

While giants of powerboat racing struggle for honors in major races and speed kings battle with high-frequency vibrations between the water and the hull of a boat at 200 miles per hour, powerboat enthusiasts keep competition lively in the slower but safer classes.

PIGEONS THAT RACE HOME

A SWARM OF PIGEONS circled above the railroad station where a railway express agent had just opened a crate of racing homers. Some continued to circle for about thirty minutes, but others headed for home almost at once.

For some of these birds, home was 200 miles away. Today their owners are thrilling to the excitement of the big race. Today is their reward for months of patient training. Some owners will be disappointed because their birds are not the winners, but they will welcome each pigeon with joy because it has reached home safely, no matter what its speed. A few of the pigeons may meet with tragedy on their long, lonely flights home. Storms, fogs, hawks, eagles, and gunners are among the hazards a pigeon may encounter.

On the whole, well-trained birds are alert and courageous. They fly fast, evading danger as they wing their way safely home.

Pigeon raising is an old, old hobby. As far back as 3000 B.C., pigeons were fed and sheltered by the Egyptians. Writers of the early books of the Bible tell of pigeons used as sacrifices and as homers. Today, the Army Signal Corps takes pride in its pigeon service. Today thousands of boys and girls and men and women raise pigeons for the hobby of racing them. The sport of pigeon racing is about fifty years old, and the object of the sport has not changed through the years. Skillful breeding and training produce birds that fly home swiftly. Season after season, some pigeon fanciers produce winners.

The pigeons you see in the park are just one of several hundred varieties which have been bred by men. Racing homers are the kind that have the best homing instinct.

Look at a pigeon loft on a race day in April. The young birds in the exercise pen were born in late January and February and will not be ready for actual racing until September. They are already being trained daily from short distances, and by November some will be flying home from a 400-mile starting point.

Here are two eggs in a nest. And here is a bird whose jealous mate has been crated and put aboard a train which carried it to a city 600 miles away. Both the eggs in the nest and a mate at home help to encourage fast homing.

Pigeons That Race Home

Note the band on one leg of each pigeon. Each pigeon is banded with a number at the age of six or seven days, and this number is his for life. The band may also show the initials of the club to which the bird belongs and perhaps the initials of his own name. They always include his date of birth.

The pigeons in this loft have bright, sparkling eyes, indicative of good health and temperament. The colors of their feathers vary greatly, and their size is average. These characteristics are not important, but eyesight and endurance are.

At dawn this morning, fifteen birds from this loft began their long flight home. Through the updrafts and downdrafts in mountain country, through blinding rain and scorching sun, they fly swiftly toward their home loft. Some encounter high wires, hawks, and falcons. Others speed straight ahead over large bodies of water, while a few stop to drink and rest because they are physically inferior.

Their speed will be measured in yards per minute and may be over 1,500 yards for one minute, or about 50 miles per hour. Fast birds may travel as much as 80 miles an hour when there is a brisk tail wind.

The liberator phones the take-off time to the secretary of the club to which this owner belongs. The secretary passes this news along to club members. As arrival time approaches, bird owners climb atop fences and roofs to watch the skies for their birds. As soon as a pigeon arrives at the loft, the owner will remove the rubber band from his leg and place it in a metal capsule. He drops this in a special clock and turns a handle to record the time. Even fractions of a second may count.

Here comes a pigeon home from the race. He is not interested in the time he made, but in returning to his mate and the eggs he left in the nest. Since he sensed pulsations in the eggs just before he was shipped away, this cock had the strongest possible desire to return home. His owner rushes to capture the band from his leg and record the time. This bird may well be a winner. This is his owner's reward for the years of breeding, for the many patient hours he spent in training, and for the wisdom he showed in timing the nesting situation. No prize is more coveted than the honor and the cup from winning a long race.

Calculating which bird is winner of a race is a complicated procedure. When pigeons are first taken to the club for shipment to the liberation point, loft owners take their special racing time clocks along so that they can be synchronized with the master clock and sealed shut. When the band is removed from a returning pigeon's leg, the owner wastes no time in inserting it into his racing clock so that the time is stamped on a tape inside.

After a race, club members gather with their clocks. Tapes are removed and the time is calculated. The distance of each loft from the starting point must be taken into consideration. Three teams of members check and recheck figures before the winner is officially announced.

In some cases, there is prize money to add to the glory of the winner.

How do racing homers find their way? There have been many answers to this question, but no one really knows which, if any, is the correct one. Some fanciers believe that pigeons can recognize landmarks and that they fly in wider and wider circles until they recognize a sight, then head toward home. It is true that pigeons fly more slowly and that there are more casualties in snowy, rainy, and foggy weather than when the sky is clear. Many untrained birds refuse to fly when the visibility is poor. And blindfolded pigeons have a poor record for homing. All this seems to indicate that eyesight plays a part in the homing instinct, but the fact remains that some pigeons which have been shipped in crates through strange regions have found their way home.

The pigeon which flew from her new home in Caracas, Venezuela, to her old home on Long Island, about 3,000 miles away, probably did not get there by watching landmarks.

Some people believe that pigeons might "tune in" to some kind of electrical air lanes. It is true that many pigeons have become confused in their route when they have flown near radar and radio broadcasting stations, but experiments have shown that pigeons do not fly "the beam" of any radio or radar stations.

The earth's magnetism has also been suggested as an answer to the question of how pigeons streak directly toward the home loft. In one experiment, tiny magnets were attached to the wings of ten homing pigeons, and tiny pieces of copper were attached to the wings of ten others in a similar way. The two groups of birds were released. Eight of the pigeons who carried the magnets lost their way, while eight of the birds carrying the copper plates returned to their lofts. However, not enough experiments have been made to prove that magnetism plays any part in the homing of pigeons, since the strong magnetic effects of mine sweepers did not bother sea birds during the war. Many fanciers think it is not even part of the answer.

Recently, scientists have suggested that pigeons may use a navigation based on the sun and brightness of the sky. If a pigeon notes that the sun is not in the position that it normally is when he sees it at home at a certain hour, he flies until the condition is remedied. This is just another idea which may or may not be true.

No matter what the explanation, thousands of racing homers speed toward their home lofts year after year. Some become confused and lose time, while others never reach home, but fanciers know that training does help. The more frequently a bird is released from varying distances from its loft, the faster it is likely to return from a race.

Racing pigeons is a fascinating hobby if one has the patience and the time to devote to it. The excitement that comes with speed, the thrill of having winners in the loft, is more than worth the effort to many people, both young and old.

FUN ON TWO WHEELS

CROWDS OF EXCITED people have gathered at the Indiana University Memorial Stadium in Bloomington, Indiana, to watch a sport that can be as thrilling as any in the world. Today college students will pedal their bicycles two hundred times around the quarter-mile cinder track which circles the field as they compete in the "Little 500," a 50-mile bicycle race.

Each year, this famous and successful race adds thousands of dollars to the scholarship fund for those who are working their way through college. Each year, the crowds feel the excitement of race day as the riders mount the bicycles for the pace lap two minutes before the starting time. Off they go in preparation for a flying start, with the order already determined by qualifying time. The rider of the fastest team takes the pole position, and thirty-two other riders fall into proper order behind the pacemaker. As the pacemaker crosses the starting line, the official starter waves the green flag, signals a clear course, and the riders are off on the grueling ride in the hot sun.

Now the actual timing and scoring begin. Each four-man team has a two-man crew waiting in the pit to provide any service to bicycles or the team's needs. Team members await their time to ride.

Teams may change riders whenever they wish, but they must do so in front of their own pits. There is quite an art to such an exchange, for the bicycle is kept rolling to prevent loss of time. The incoming rider drops off the saddle, holds it while running to push the bike ahead to the relief rider. The latter grasps the handle bars and makes a flying leap to the saddle. If the incoming rider fails to start the exchange in front of his own pit, he must make another lap before attempting to make the change.

A broken bicycle brings excited action to a pit, where the mechanic rushes to make the necessary repairs and get the bicycle back into the race. Other pit action includes the exercising of reserve riders on roller bikes so that their muscles are limber when they rush onto the saddle of a moving bike.

Now and then a yellow flag signals an accident and prevents riders from trying to better their positions until the injured rider is rescued or the broken bicycle removed from the track. After a yellow flag has been shown, a green flag signals a clear track.

All eyes are watching for the white flag to signal the start of the last lap. The crowd roars as the winner wheels across the finish line and takes the checkered flag at the end of the 50-mile grind. He circles the track for one more lap, then leaves it for the infield so that he may appear in the winner's circle. Other teams are flagged for their finish, their time is recorded, and they remain in their pits until called.

Such a race is a success for losers as well as for winners, for all have a fine time enjoying the spirit of good sportsmanship and the satisfaction of knowing their hard work of training and organizing the race will help boys and girls to complete their college educations. Whether riding for a cause or just for fun, bicycle racing is a good sport.

One of the most famous bicycle races in the United States is the annual Tour of Sommerville, held each Memorial Day in Sommerville, New Jersey. Teams of cyclists from many parts of the world come to compete in this "Kentucky Derby" of bicycle racing.

Each summer, the most famous bicycle race in the world takes place in France. The Tour of France is a terrific test of endurance for those teams of cyclists who travel over approximately 3,000 miles during a period of twenty-five to thirty days. About a hundred men begin the course that winds its way through as many as a hundred communities, over cold mountain peaks as high as 7,000 feet, and through hot streets of southern France.

Imagine pumping a bicycle up a mountain into the

midst of a low-hanging cloud, twisting almost blindly around the curves until you reach the top. Next comes the downhill run on which the cyclist can relax only until his speed becomes dangerous. He must be expert at judging his degree of braking so that he can make speed but avoid spills. Spills are common in the Tour of France. Many riders finish with scrapes and bruises, and some are forced to stop after bicycles pile up in a jam when one rider in the pack meets with an accident. But most of them move swiftly over the long course toward Paris amidst the clouds of dust which they stir from the road. Many of them average as much as 25 miles per hour.

Advertising displays on trucks, vans, automobiles, and motorcycles that follow the race, paid testimonials from riders, and prizes and publicity supplied by businessmen have made the race a noisy affair which some sportsmen have compared to a medicine show. But in spite of this, winning the Tour of France is still considered the highest honor in cycling. Excitement is high along the course where spectators watch for the famous yellow jersey which is worn by the cyclist who is the leader. He may not be ahead of all riders at every point on the course, for almost each day starts a new stage and there is a winner for each stage, but he is the over-all leader. The yellow jersey of leadership may be worn by many different riders before the race is over, but the one who wears it in the last lap is the winner. He has won fame and money, and will be honored in many ways by the people who watch the race and read about it with great interest. Even schoolteachers in France have used the Tour of France to make subjects such as geology, geography, history, and arithmetic more interesting. In France, this cycling race has been called a "national institution," and all over the world, sports enthusiasts keep posted on its progress.

Six-day bicycle racing continues to flourish in Europe, but in the United States interest since World War II has been largely with shorter amateur races. Throughout the country, road, dirt-track, and board races are sponsored by various organizations. The Elgin-Chicago Race is the oldest of the present-day classics. Each year the "Best All 'Rounder Competition" is sponsored by the Bicycle Institute of America, and a champion of bicycle road racing is determined on a point basis for a number of sponsored races.

One interesting type of indoor racing popular during the winter season is roller racing, in which training bicycles are pedaled on rollers. A dial which records progress lights up, showing spectators how the men are "riding."

In any season of the year, you and your friends can enjoy the fun which comes with the activities of a neighborhood bicycle club. If you would like help in forming such a club, write to the Bicycle Institute of America, 122 East 42d Street, New York 17, New York, for suggestions on how to organize, draw up a constitution, plan activities, and promote an active bicycle club which will bring enjoyment to every member.

You might plan a bicycle day with a program of races which include the usual and open handicap races and some of the following variations.

Try a race in which the winner is the last one across the finish line. If a foot touches the ground, the contestant is disqualified.

A pursuit race is exciting. Riders are placed at equal distances from each other along the course. If one rider is passed by another, he is out of the race. This race continues until there is only one left.

For the following three races, chalk courses are drawn, and individual riders are timed with stop watches, since they travel the course one at a time.

Parallel-line races provide a great deal of fun for riders and spectators alike. Draw two parallel lines about 3 feet apart over a distance of 75 feet. To do

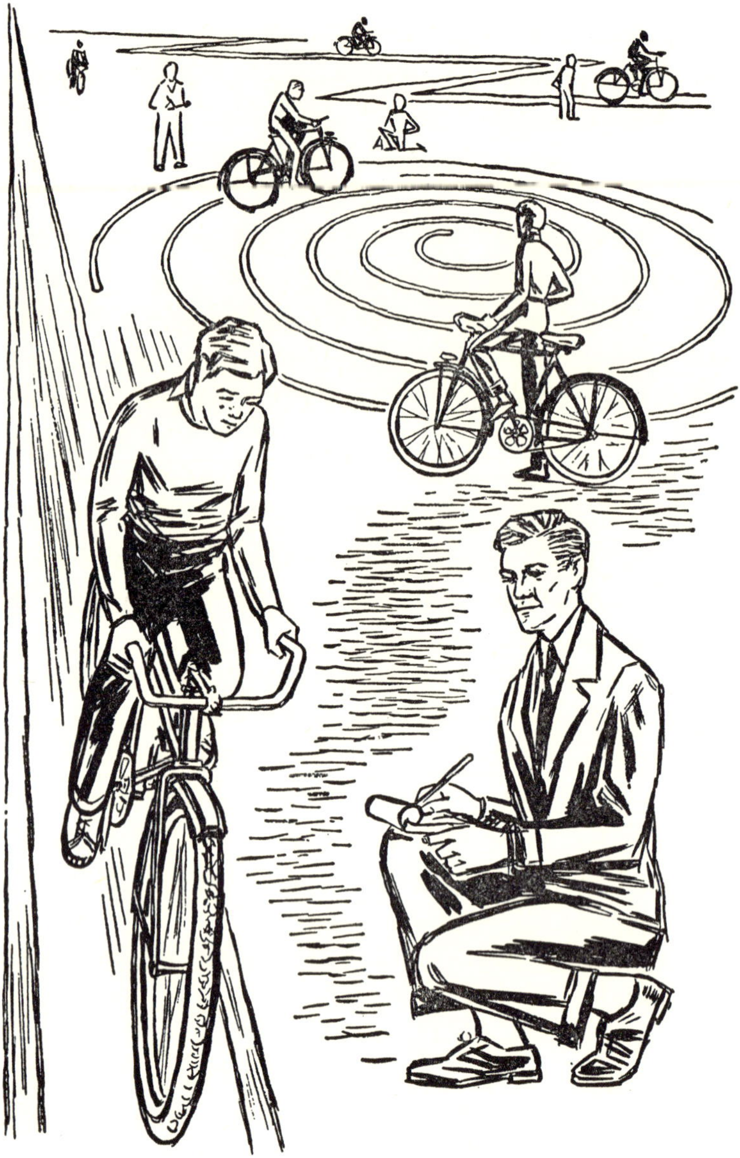

this, cut a string 3½ feet long and tie chalk to each end. Have two people walk over the course marking it with the chalk as they go.

A variation of this is the bicycle *slalom,* in which lines are zigzag and 5 feet apart. Draw parallel lines on one angle for 20 or 25 feet, then make an angle and mark 20 more feet. Continue in this manner until you have completed a course to your liking. If a contestant rides on a chalk line, he is disqualified.

A chalked spiral is another version of bicycle racing. To mark the course, prepare a piece of string 20 feet long with a stick of chalk tied on one end. Have one person hold the chalk while the other holds the opposite end of the string at the place which will be the center of the circle. This person gradually pulls in the string as the marker chalks the spiral.

Obstacle, relays, and other team races provide almost endless variations of this wonderful sport.

You might invite officers or members of civic groups to act as starter, scorers, and timers for your race program. There should be at least two pairs of scorers, with one calling numbers of riders and one recording them, in each pair. Timers should work in pairs, too, one calling out the elapsed time as the rider crosses the finish line, and the other recording it. When time sheets and score sheets are brought together, a referee can determine the order of finish. Scorers and timers should work on both sides of the finish line.

Many manufacturers and dealers of bicycles have

designed trophies and medals as prizes for winners of bicycle-club races. These may be available to your group if your club has been accredited by the Bicycle Institute of America. Local merchants and civic groups may help, too.

The Amateur Bicycle League of America, whose object is to foster bicycle racing under the leadership of bicycle clubs, is the official governing body of organized bicycle racing in the United States. Each year, racing championships are run off first in each state. Winners are sent to the national championship race with expenses paid by bicycle manufacturers. These races have been held in many parts of the United States and include competitions for boys over seventeen years of age in one-half-, one-and-a-half-, and ten-mile events, and for younger ones in the junior class in one-half-mile, one-mile, and five-mile events. Girls' races are usually one-half mile and one mile in length.

Olympic tryouts are held every four years and provide exciting competition for experts. You need not make the Olympic team to have fun on wheels. In sprint races, in cross-country record runs, in local bicycle-club races, and in world championships, riding your best and showing good sportsmanship are the important things.

Motorcycles

In contrast to bicycle racing, which promotes health and safe speeding, is the sport of motorcycle racing, which

Fun on Two Wheels

remains popular among a group of rugged men who are willing to risk injuries and even death for thrills and prize money.

The American Motorcycle Association, which makes the rules for all recognized motorcycle competitions prohibits any rider under twenty-one from entering a race unless he has the written consent of his parents or legal guardian. No women of any age may compete in hill climbs or any races which involve speed as a determining factor. The association also insists that racers wear leather pants to protect them from pavement burns in case of a fall. Sliding over a distance of concrete or dirt surface on his back or stomach is a common experience for a motorcycle racer. A layer of leather between skin and the road makes the slide less painful.

In spite of the hazards, those who participate in motorcycle events are extremely enthusiastic about their sport. Hill climbing, popularly called "shooting the slant," provides thrills for those who watch as well as for those who ride. In a series of trials against time, distance, or both, riders take backflips and spills as a matter of course.

Practice runs up the steep slopes are forbidden, so motorcyclists may be seen walking up the hill before the race looking for holes, bumps, or spots of loose earth on the upgrade and making a mental note of what they will run through when they reach the top. There may be trees, cliffs, rocks, or any other natural obstruction on the other side, and when a rider comes over the top he is going at high speed.

The course uphill is a narrow trail just 20 or 25 feet in width, and the rider must stay on the course. He must gather speed for the climb on a flat space about 30 feet long and then try to surmount a hill that seems to rise almost straight up from the ground. Some are so steep that riders have tried year after year before one gets over the top. Even though no one conquers a hill, there is still a winner, for one will reach a higher spot than the others. The distance scored is the highest point reached by the rear wheel of the motorcycle while the rider is

Fun on Two Wheels

still in contact with the machine. He need not be sitting on it. Each racer is allowed three trials, and there are runoffs in case of ties in this rugged sport where bad spills and somersaults are all part of the game.

Another motorcycle event which involves speed is racing on dirt tracks. Thousands of fans gather at the tracks to watch racers roar around the course in their plastic helmets, colorful jerseys, and leather pants. Metal plates on the soles of their shoes serve as brakes when drivers grind them against the dirt of the track to slow themselves at curves. Those who make a living by capturing the prize money at such events must work hard and ride well. They must travel from city to city to enter the big events at Reading, Pennsylvania; Springfield, Illinois; Dodge City, Kansas; Atlanta, Georgia; Catalina, California; and at other tracks from coast to coast.

The most outstanding event in motorcycling is the 200-mile national championship which is held every year at Daytona Beach, Florida. This is a combination beach and road race over a 4.1-mile course on which riders make 49 laps. Usually the beach stretch is smooth, but wind may make ripples, so that riders may find rough traveling over a surface that is somewhat like a washboard. Nearly every year the caution flag must fly to protect a spilled cyclist until he and his machine are removed from the track. Every year motorcyclists aim for higher and higher speeds over this famous course of sand and macadam straightaways and turns that are cut from the dunes and banked with rock and clay. This race at Daytona Beach ranks with the most famous in the world.

The Tourist Trophy Road Race on the Isle of Man is probably the most famous motorcycle race of all time. On this island in the Irish Sea, men from more than a dozen countries compete. This and six other championships contribute points toward the International Grand Prix Title. "Tourist" as used in the title, Tourist Trophy Race, is a word which describes a class of motorcycles which are stock motorcycles, the kind listed in catalogues for ordinary road travel. They are not as fast as those specially designed for racing and are less dangerous. Today many people feel that even tourist motorcycles have become too fast for competitions for all but the most highly skilled riders. With the existing accident rate

Fun on Two Wheels

for motorcycle racing, it is quite possible that a smaller, slower class of cycles will be recognized.

Tourist trophy races are races over a prepared course, no part of which is a traveled road. There are a number of laps over a closed course which has both uphill and downhill stretches and both right and left turns.

Races with sidecars, races on board tracks, and races on roads which are closed for the occasion are also sanctioned by the American Motorcycle Association. Drag races, races in which two men compete or in which one races against time, are popular in some sections of the country. In addition to the motorcycles in speed competitions, there are endurance runs, economy runs, cross-country runs, and other types of tours on motorcycles. To the men who ride and the people who watch, these are ways of having fun on wheels in spite of the hazards.

FAST WINGS

SPEED IS KING in many flights. From tiny model planes to the giants that streak through the sky, the quest for speed goes on. Here are some glimpses into the world of fast wings where some play and others experiment in strange ways.

A model airplane meet bustles with fun and excitement. About 400 model airplane competitions are sanctioned each year by the Academy of Model Aeronautics. Thousands of people gather together to watch and participate in outstanding contests such as those held in Detroit, Michigan, and Bethpage, Long Island, New York, where champions fly their models. Young people come from every state in the nation and from some foreign countries for the "World Series" of model aviation, the

Fast Wings

National Model Airplane Championships, which are held each year in different localities.

If you have been crowned winner in local and regional meets, you might be sent to the Nationals and quartered at the Naval Air Station where the contest will be held. You will thrill to the tremendous air show featuring the Navy's Blue Angels and flight demonstrations of some of the country's newest jet aircraft. You will compete with the very best when you fly your model.

Many model events do not emphasize speed, but a few do. You might fasten the steel control line of your gas-powered model to a fixed pivot post, known as a pylon, and watch it whiz around so fast that it may reach a speed of 150 miles an hour. Or you might stand in the center of the flight circle, by the pylon, and hold the control handle attached to the wires which are fastened to the model. You avoid "leading" the plane by resting your hand on the pylon and control the model by wrist movement. Spectators who are watching behind a protective wire screen gasp as they see your plane gain speed. Excitement mounts as the timers click their stop watches and begin to count the six laps which make the half-mile course. But even if you win this event, such speed may not be the top for the meet.

Another type of control-line model plane may be faster because it has an internal-combustion engine connected to a tail pipe through which burned gases shoot. The jet model moves forward as exhaust gases rush out from explosions which may take place at a rate of 230 times a second. Imagine the roar when these jet models reach a speed as great as 170 miles per hour. The young people who master such model techniques began with simple models and worked gradually into the art of flying fast model planes. Many will continue their aviation careers to become outstanding pilots and airplane designers. Many who join the search for better speed for today's planes began their work as model-plane enthusiasts.

Some young people will join the pilots who race their planes from one airfield to another. In addition to the fun of the race and the chance of winning cash and trophy prizes, there are owners of light planes who participate in many local and some national events to encourage transportation with private planes.

One air classic is the annual All-Woman Transcontinental Air Race which is flown over a 2,000-mile course from the West to the East of the United States. Imagine approximately fifty polished and glistening planes tuned to wrist-watch precision standing ready for take-off. Although the race is popularly known as the Powder-puff Derby, few women pilots and copilots are concerned with their makeup when an official waves the starting flag and the first plane rolls down the runway. The remaining planes take off in rapid order.

Pilots must travel over a planned route between the hours of sunrise and sunset, and each one has to select the altitude which will make her plane most efficient and make the most of the uncontrollable factors of wind and weather. Each pilot hopes for speed that will make her a winner.

The Jaycee Transcontinental Handicap Air Cruise is a cross-country race for men who pilot light planes. Some of the pilots spend much of their leisure time flying and keeping their planes in tune for the big race. Rules are similar to those for the women's race, with certain check points that must be covered and racing time based on actual time in flight. The tired pilots who turn in their flight logs and gas tickets at the end of the race wait eagerly for news from the committee. Each one hopes for the glory of being the over-all winner or winner for his class of plane.

Famous trophies are awarded each year to speed kings who fly jet planes for the Armed Forces at the National Air Shows. In addition to the men who break records for the Thompson Trophy, the General Electric Trophy, and the Bendix Trophy, many jet pilots search for greater speed in their everyday work. At Edwards Air Force Base on Muroc Lake, California, the dry lake bed makes an ideal landing strip for their secret tests. Here in the Mojave Desert, about a hundred miles northeast of Los Angeles, new planes fly above the prickly cactus. Here, far from civilization, Capt. Charles Yeager was the first man to fly faster than the speed of sound.

In addition to protecting military secrets, the distance from civilization has another advantage. If you spend a few days at Muroc Lake, you will soon hear why. The sky may be clear and bright when thunderlike noises reach your ears. You may not see the plane which streaks through the sky, but you will soon learn that the boom comes from one that has crashed through the sonic barrier.

Each time a jet travels as fast as or faster than the speed of sound, it sets waves of air in motion. These

Fast Wings

waves are pressure waves or shock waves which can be compared to the surface waves of water created when a motorboat travels on a still lake. Under certain weather conditions, the shock waves reach the ground and strike it with such impact that an explosive noise is heard. Sonic boom has broken windows and small beams of wood, it has knocked down some people and frightened many more, but it is not otherwise dangerous to those who hear its ghostlike noises.

Although sonic boom cannot be completely prevented, much has been done to keep it away from residential districts. Most of the thunderlike blasts come from diving planes, and most are not heard because pilots are instructed to carry out their dives over oceans or deserts where the shock waves they set in motion will not reach buildings and people. Planes which travel faster than the speed of sound in level flight might set up a boom which could trail along like a shadow after the plane to annoy everyone in its path, but such planes fly at high levels over residential areas so that their sonic boom will probably never reach your ears.

The problems of sonic boom are being studied at many places, but there is still much to be learned about it and about what might happen to light planes if they try to pierce the sound barrier. Some experts believe they might split apart. Another problem of high speed in the sky is the heat or thermal barrier. As jets rush through the air, molecules of air become hot from friction. Some of this heat is transferred to the skin of the plane. Special cooling devices prevent the wings of supersonic planes from melting like wax.

Until new materials are developed or new systems of cooling a plane's skin are perfected, there is a limit to how fast man can fly in air. Pilots speak of speed in relation to the speed of sound in terms of "Mach." Mach 1 is the speed of sound, Mach 2 is twice that speed, and so on. At Mach 4, the shock wave created by a plane would heat its metallic skin to a temperature ten times as hot as that of boiling water. Aluminum melts at Mach 5, steel at Mach 6, and at Mach 10, 7,600 miles per hour, even a diamond would be transformed into a puff or vapor. There is extensive research for new materials which will go into tomorrow's fast planes. Among other materials, glass fabric is being studied.

The pilot of the X-15, a research craft built to fly above the earth's atmosphere, has been described as a man in a hot metal tube. The solving of heat problems is the key to the design of the X-15.

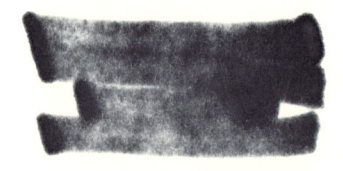

In his endless quest for speed, man is his own greatest enemy, for he was not made to live high above the treetops. If you sit in the cockpit of a plane in which you hope to break through the sound barrier, you will be practically "built into" the machine for your protection. Ten different lines will connect you to equipment such as radar, oxygen supply, radio and heat controls, parachute, and seat. Your flight suit will have special pressure chambers in the stomach area and in the regions of your legs to lessen the effects of increased pressure which you will experience.

Your crash helmet will be adjusted so that microphones and headphones are connected, and the plastic visor will be electrically heated to prevent frosting. A little red light which will give you warning of an insufficient supply of oxygen before your body notices the lack is part of the device known as a "brain-wave writer." When all your equipment has been checked and is in perfect working order, a Plexiglas hood will be pushed over your head. The ground crew will be alert in front of numerous instruments when the screaming noise of your jet engine begins and you roll down the concrete runway to rise through the blue into the dark sky above it.

Without protection, at 55,000 feet you would become unconscious in 13 seconds. Keeping a pilot safe under the stress of high altitude and speed is the task of space and aviation medicine, a fascinating field. At the Aerospace Medical Center, Brooks Air Force Base, Texas, and a number of laboratories throughout the United States, scientists are trying to learn how human beings can keep pace with the great strides made in plane development by aviation engineers.

Some exciting experiments are being made in strange-looking merry-go-rounds, called centrifuges, to learn more about man's reaction to high speed and acceleration. Suppose you have volunteered to participate in a project at the U.S. Naval Air Development Center at Johnsville, Pennsylvania, in the world's largest human centrifuge. The purpose of the experiment is to learn more about what happens when pilots lose their vision, or black out, under certain conditions of high speed. It is obvious that a pilot's heart must pump blood *up* to his eyes while he is sitting upright. When his heart is under stress and cannot function properly because of changes in direction or speed in a fast plane, is his vision blacked out because of lack of blood in the back of the brain or in the back of the eye itself?

You sit in a special platform on the 50-foot arm of the huge centrifuge. A powerful motor which weighs 180 tons can spin you from a standstill to 180 miles per hour in less than 7 seconds. Your speed will be controlled by an operator who will watch you from a glass observation booth which hangs from the ceiling.

When you are spinning, your reactions will be studied

Fast Wings

through the use of television and movie cameras. High-speed X rays will record the effects on your heart, lungs and other organs. Instruments fastened to your body pick up reactions which are recorded on long strips of paper that move in front of the eyes of watchful scientists in a room above the centrifuge.

You will black out in the experiment, but the doctor who is studying your eyes must spin with you and still be in such physical condition that he can observe them. To prevent his blacking out, the doctor will ride in a horizontal position so that his heart does not have to pump blood up to his head. In this position, the human body can better tolerate acceleration.

After long days of preparation, everyone is ready for the first test run. Your harness and lap belt have been fastened, wires which will record reactions have been connected, and your eyes have been treated with medicine that will enable the doctor to watch changes in them.

The centrifuge whizzes around. Now you cannot see the lights which shine on both sides of you because you have reached a stage of gray-out. The stress of acceleration continues, and the light directly in front of you seems to dim and disappear. You have blacked out, but you are still conscious. You can still answer a buzzer by moving your finger. Now the machine swings faster. You become completely unconscious.

This run is just the beginning of the experiment. To answer this one question about the changes causing blackout, ten volunteers rode in the centrifuge. One, Howard Hunter, who is chief engineer of the laboratory, rode day after day while the apparatus was being perfected. He made fifty runs while a medical artist made observations which enabled him to draw pictures of what happened in his eyes. All this led to the answer of just one question. Changes take place in the back of the eye when a pilot blacks out. Here is another bit of knowledge which will help the men who work to protect pilots.

Day after day tests go on to explore the limits of human tolerance to acceleration, to develop protective equipment, and to learn more about the ability of pilots to perform under stress of high speed and acceleration. There

Fast Wings

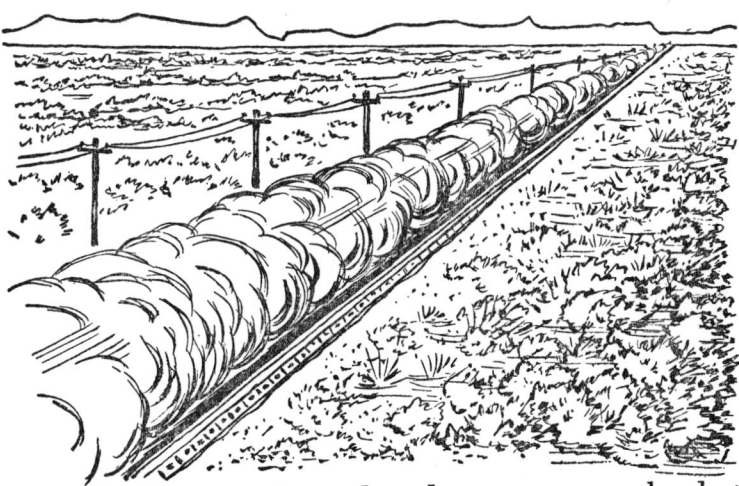

is much more to be learned, and many men are hard at work trying to find the answers.

On the flat sands of Holloman Air Development Center in New Mexico, Col. John Paul Stapp made history when he sped down the rails on a sled at 623 miles per hour in December of 1954. This broke all speed records for land travel.

Strapped to a rocket-propelled sled that traveled over iron rails, Colonel Stapp was propelled at a speed which increased for a distance of half a mile during a period of five seconds. Then the sled coasted at record speed for one-half second and was brought to a dead stop in a fraction more than a second. The wind force against his body when he reached top speed was equivalent to that of almost 1.7 times the speed of sound (more than 1,000 miles per hour) at 35,000 feet, the normal cruising altitude for jet aircraft.

A nylon web harness held Colonel Stapp in place during the quick stop, but his eyeballs were thrown against his eyelids so hard that he suffered two black eyes. With the exception of these and blood blisters from dust particles in the air, the test produced no ill effects.

This test was a highlight in a series of experiments on the effects of high-speed travel on the human body. Although most of the problems are directed toward military developments, there are safety applications for commercial airliners. For instance, Colonel Stapp has added further proof to the theory that backward-facing seats in aircraft provide a maximum of safety with a minimum of harness. Persons seated facing the rear of a plane can withstand forces that might snap the harness of a person facing forward. Such seats might save many lives when airplanes crash.

The quest for speed goes on. Who knows how fast tomorrow's atomic planes and space ships may travel and what new problems they may bring?

SPEEDING INTO SPACE

THE MEN WHO RUN, the men who speed through the snow on skis, even the men who drive fast cars are slow travelers compared with those who streak through the sky in fast planes. And, even the planes are slow compared with the rockets of today and the space ships that may carry men to the moon and planets beyond the earth in years to come. Some of today's rockets have reached speeds as great as 25,000 miles per hour. At such speed, they escape from the earth and coast forever in orbit around the sun.

Speed is important in the world of space today. Sometime in the future, atomic engines may be able to reach into space more slowly with a steady thrust of power that will last a long time, but with the chemical rockets that are now climbing into the sky, jack rabbit starts are needed. With chemical rockets, the fuel is completely used in reaching escape velocity, about 25,000 miles per hour, and the rocket coasts without fuel for the rest of its trip.

Here is an idea which may help you to better understand what is meant by escape velocity. Suppose you throw a ball high into the air. No matter how hard you throw it, the ball will come back to the earth. It comes down because of gravity, a mysterious force which pulls the ball, you, and everything else toward the center of the earth. The earth's gravity pulls so hard that even the best baseball player in the world could not throw a ball high enough or fast enough to make it escape from the earth.

Suppose you use a rocket to toss a "scientific ball" high in the sky. This is the way satellites are carried into orbit. Imagine an earth satellite being borne spaceward on a tremendous "golden jet" that shoots from the base of a three-stage rocket. The giant rocket lights up the night with a seething burst of flame. Gradually it rises from the launching pad. As it gains speed, the rocket gives off a violent roar. It rises higher and higher as a steadily smaller spark burning its way out of sight in the starry blue sky.

Speeding into Space

The first stage drops off, a second ignites, and the speed increases. Now the second stage is burned out, and a third carries the ball into the sky and puts it in the proper angle to travel around the earth.

And so with a speed of about 18,000 miles per hour, the ball begins to travel around the earth. This ball was not shot into the sky fast enough to continue its journey away from the earth. Its rocket motors are spent, and the pull of the earth's gravity takes over. But, the satellite is traveling so fast that it does not fall back to the earth. This ball falls *around* the earth. It is a satellite in orbit. You can show how this happens by taking a rubber ball attached to a long piece of string and swinging it around you. When you swing it fast enough, the ball will not fall to the ground, but will swing out at right angles to your body.

Some satellites travel around the earth in less than a hundred minutes, while others take more time. Those satellites near the earth where the pull of gravity is strong must travel very fast so that gravity does not pull them back. The moon, our natural satellite, can stay in its path at a slower speed, because it is so far away. And, there is no air so far from the earth to slow the moon in its path. It does not lose speed and fall back to earth as many other satellites do.

How fast must a ball be tossed into the sky to escape the earth's attraction and coast forever in space? Scientists have long known that escape velocity is about 25,000 miles per hour, but only recently have they been able to reach that tremendous speed. The first rocket to reach escape velocity was *Lunik,* the Russian missile which was launched on January 2, 1959. Scientists around the world were excited as they listened to the signals of *Lunik* rushing toward the moon. Past the moon it went, about 5,000 miles from its surface. This is a short distance compared with the 239,000 miles between the earth and moon. On went the rocket toward the sun to take its place as the first artificial planet in the solar system.

Many things were needed to put a rocket into orbit around the sun. One of the most important of these was speed. And so it was with the first American rocket that reached escape velocity. The first Pioneer rockets failed to reach enough speed to escape, but *Pioneer IV* left its launching pad on March 3, 1959, and lunged in the direction of the moon. Faster and faster it traveled until it reached the speed of about 24,800 miles per hour. As it climbed toward the moon, *Pioneer IV* was gradually slowed by the tug of the earth's gravity, but its top speed was great enough to send it beyond the power of the earth's attraction. It passed the moon at a distance of 37,000 miles, and went into orbit around the sun at a speed of about 4,000 miles per hour. Here, along with the first Russian satellite, it will circle the sun as long as the earth and other planets in the solar system, unless smashed by a chance meteor. Such a collision seems unlikely.

Space men look forward to a trip to the moon before

they hope to orbit around the sun. From a space station that is already speeding 18,000 miles per hour around the earth, the ship will need an additional velocity of 7,000 miles per hour in the early part of a moon journey.

What about trips to planets such as Mars and Venus? Mars, in its most favorable position, is 35 million miles away. When men know how to steer, and have solved many other problems of space flight, they may make the trip in 259 days with a starting velocity of 7.2 miles per second (25,920 miles per hour). After the rockets are burned out, a space ship may coast to Mars at a speed of 1.8 miles per second (6,480 miles per hour). Compare this speed with other speeds described in the earlier chapters of this book.

A journey to Venus might begin with a space ship reaching a peak velocity of 7.14 miles per second (25,700 miles per hour) and last for 146 days. Other planets are even farther away. Imagine the speeds involved in trips to distant planets. Venus is sometimes 25 million miles away, while Pluto is at least 3½ billion miles from the earth.

Space scientists talk of trips even beyond the solar system. Will the length of the journey to a star be longer than a human life span? Rocket men talk about a space ship propelled by shooting unbelievably concentrated beams of light from its tail. In such a way they may obtain speeds almost as great as the speed of light, which is 186,000 miles per second. Even at this speed, a round trip to the star Alpha Centauri would take about nine years. Except for the sun, this is the star nearest to the earth.

Many scientists believe that time slows down for a person traveling in a space ship at a speed near that of light. They say that clocks on space ships would not run as fast as clocks back on earth. But unless a space man could compare time on the space ship with time on the earth, he would not sense the slowing of time.

Will space travelers age more slowly than men back on the earth? Will a man who leaves his twin brother at home find that he is younger than the twin when he returns from a long trip in space? This has been the subject of much debate among scientists. No one knows the answer. Perhaps they will not know until men travel through space at near the speed of light, in a space ship where speed is king.

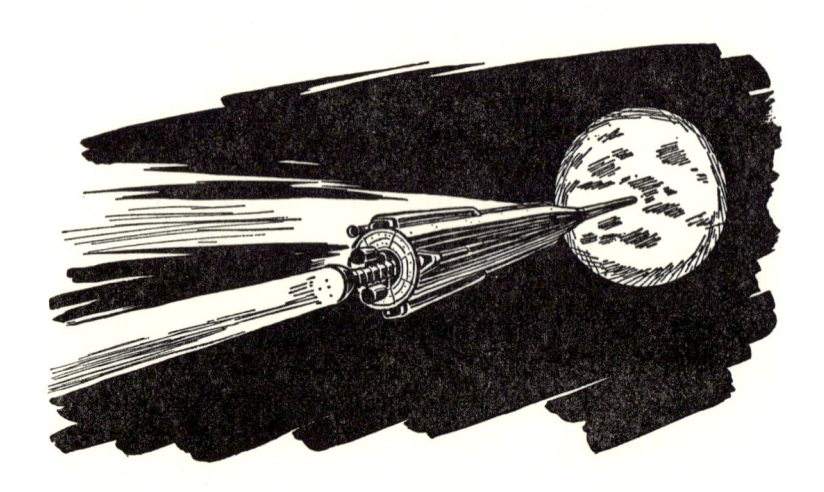

OFFICIAL SPORTS ORGANIZATIONS

The organizations listed below may be able to provide you with various kinds of information on speed records, how to form a club, how to participate in organized races, and where races are held.

SWIMMING AND TRACK

Amateur Athletic Union
233 Broadway
New York 7, New York

HORSE RACING

Thoroughbred Racing Associations of the United States, Inc.
925 Chrysler Building
New York 17, New York

U.S. Trotting Association
1349 E. Broad Street
Columbus, Ohio

WINTER SPORTS

Amateur Athletic Union of the United States (bobsledding)
233 Broadway, New York 7, New York

American Dog Derby Incorporated
West Yellowstone, Montana

International Renegade Ice Yacht Association
Mrs. Cora Lee Millenbach, Secretary
8068 Lamphere Street, Detroit 39, Michigan

Skate-Sailing Association of America
150 Nassau Street, Room 1428
New York 38, New York

National Ski Association of America
1130 Sixteenth Street
Denver 2, Colorado

SOAP BOX AND AUTOMOBILE RACING

All-American Soap Box Derby, Inc.
General Motors Building
Detroit 2, Michigan

National Hot Rod Association
1171 North Vermont Avenue
Los Angeles 28, California

United States Auto Club
Post Office Box 24001
Speedway 24, Indiana

WATER SPORTS

National Association of Amateur Oarsmen
Mr. Francis Ludwig, Secretary
507 West 67th Avenue, Philadelphia 26, Pennsylvania

Model Yacht Racing Association of America
Mr. C. O. Davis, Secretary
6521 Fremont, Seattle 3, Washington

International Model Power Boat Association
2991 Garland Avenue, Detroit 14, Michigan

North American Yacht Racing Union
37 West 44th Street, New York 36, New York

American Power Boat Association
700 Canton Avenue, Detroit 7, Michigan

American Water Ski Association
307 N. Michigan Avenue, Chicago 1, Illinois

CYCLING

Amateur Bicycle League of America
% Otto Eisle
2320 Grand Avenue
New York 68, New York

American Motorcycle Association
106 Buttles Avenue
Columbus, Ohio

AIRPLANES

Academy of Model Aeronautics
1025 Connecticut Avenue
Washington 6, D.C.

National Aeronautic Association
1025 Connecticut Avenue
Washington 6, D.C.

INDEX

Academy of Model Aeronautics, 122
Air races, 124–126
Amateur Bicycle League, 116
American Power Boat Association, 92–93
Athlete's heart, 8–11
Automobile Racing Hall of Fame, 70
Aviation medicine, 129–134

Bannister, Roger, 7–9, 11
Bicycle Institute of America, 112–113
Bicycle racing, 108–116
Bobsledding, 26–30
Boston Marathon, 15

Campbell, Donald, 100
Cobb, John, 58
Cresta toboggan run, 23–25
Cross-country running, 15
Cunningham, Briggs, 63, 64
Cunningham, Glenn, 12
Cureton, Thomas K., 9–11

Dog-sled racing, 30–34

Elliot, Herb, 8, 9
English Henley, 75–76
Escape velocity, 136–137

Gold Cup, 98–100
Grand Prix cars, 68–70
Gravity, 136

Halberg, Murray, 12
Harmsworth Trophy, 99
Harness racing, 52–53
Horses, 44–53
Hot rods, 57–59
Hurdling, 15–16

Ice skating, 18–20
Ice yachting, 39–41
Indianapolis 500, 67–69
International Model Power Boat Association, 76

Landy, John, 7–9
Le Mans, 64–66, 70

Mach, 128
Mile of the Century, 7–8, 11, 12
Model airplanes, 121–123
Model power boats, 76–77
Model Yacht Racing Association of America, 79
Model yachts, 77–80
Motorcycle racing, 115–121

National Association of Stock Car Automobile Racing, 59–61

143

National Outboard Association, 92

Ocean racing, 87
Olympics, and bicycling, 116
   and bobsledding, 28
   and hurdling, 15
   and skiing, 22

Pan American Road Race, 65–67
Physical fitness and running, 8–12
Pigeons, 101–107
Predicted-log contests, 90–91
President's Cup, 97

Rockets, 135–138
Roller racing, 113
Rowing, 71–76
Running, 7–16

Safety, and automobile racing, 60–69
   and bicycling, 116–117
   and bobsledding, 27
   and coasting, 25–26
   and hot rods, 57–59
   and powerboats, 93
Safety, and water skiing, 94
Sailing, 80–87

Satellites, 136–138
Sayres, Stanley, 98–100
Silver Cup, 97
Skate-sailing, 20–22
Skiing, 34–39, 41–42
Skijoring, 39
Slalom, 37–39, 95
Soap-box racers, 54–57
Sonic boom, 125–127
Space, 135
Space ships, 139–140
Speed skating, 18–20
Sports cars, 62–67
Stapp, John Paul, 133–134
Steeplechase, 15, 52
Swimming, 16

Thompson, Mickey, 58
Thoroughbreds, 44–51
Tobogganing, 22–26
Tour of France, 110–112
Tour of Sommerville, 110

U.S. Auto Club, 61–62

Wallet, Gene, III, 85
Water skiing, 94–97
Wood, Gar, 99

Yaeger, Charles, 126

Zaharias, Babe Didrikson, 15